SAFE AT HOME

BOB MUZIKOWSKI

WITH GREGG LEWIS

SAFE AT HOME

THE TRUE AND INSPIRING STORY OF CHICAGO'S FIELD OF DREAMS

ZONDERVAN™

GRAND RAPIDS, MICHIGAN 49530

To the Friends of Bill Wilson:

Other people have profitted greatly by telling my story or variations of it in book, video, and screenplay form. After much consideration and prayer, I feel compelled to set the record straight, tell my own story, and benefit the community by doing so.

ZONDERVAN™

Safe at Home
Copyright © 2001 by Robert Muzikowski

Requests for information should be addressed to:

Zondervan, *Grand Rapids, Michigan 49530*

ISBN 0-310-24107-3

This edition printed on acid-free paper.

Author royalties will go to Chicago Hope Academy and other urban charities. Chicago Hope Academy contributions are matched by the Vranos Foundation.

Interior design by Todd Sprague

Printed in the United States of America

01 02 03 04 05 06 07 / ❖ DC/ 10 9 8 7 6 5 4 3 2 1

For Tina,
my wife, best friend,
and ultimate volunteer

And to all the volunteers
whose blood, sweat, and tears
line the fields of this country

CONTENTS

Preach the Gospel at all times.
If necessary, use words.

THE CALL

A loud ringing jarred me out of a deep sleep. *It can't be morning yet!* I opened my eyes. It's too dark! The bedside alarm clock said one something. When the phone rang again, Isaiah, my seven-month-old son, jerked and cried out from the bassinet beside our bed.

I was now fully awake and not at all happy about it. *Which one of my guys is calling me at this hour?* I wondered as I snatched up the receiver expecting to hear the sorry, wasted voice of some backslidden AA buddy. I was primed to launch into a short lecture about needing to call me *before* going out on a bender, not at 2 A.M. oozing penitence and self-pity on the pay phone from the back of some seedy bar, crying, "Poor me ... poor me ... pour me another drink." *C'mon, man! I've got a wife and three kids now.*

The moment I put the receiver to my ear, however, I could hear another child crying in the background and then a woman's hushed and sober tone. "Coach Bob, is Brian with you?"

I recognized the caller's voice right away. It belonged to Antoinette Dixon, the aunt of the first baseman on one of the Little

League teams I sponsored and coached. Her question seemed reasonable enough because Brian sometimes spent the night at our house or with a doctor friend who helped coach our team.

But not this time.

"I'm sorry, Ms. Dixon," I replied. "Brian's not here. I haven't seen him since practice last night."

"I already called Coach Bill's place, but wasn't nobody home," she told me.

I suspected Bill Vranos was on call at Cook County or one of the other hospitals where he worked as part of his orthopedic residency program. Bill's wife, Cathy, was probably out of town on business.

"The police be at the door wantin' to know is this where Brian lives," Ms. Dixon continued in a hushed voice. "I don't know what's goin' on."

I now understood why she was whispering. She obviously assumed her nephew was in trouble and had called me before she opened the door and talked to the policemen.

"It'll be all right, Ms. Dixon," I assured her. "Talk to the cops. Find out why they are looking for Brian. If they have him in custody, be sure to ask where. Then call me back and I'll go with you to get him."

Antoinette Dixon apologized for disturbing me. I told her, "Don't worry about it. Call me back if there's anything I can do."

I patted Isaiah's back for a while after I hung up. *What could Brian have done?* He wasn't one to make trouble. He lived in Gangster Disciples territory, and the GDs were feuding with the Mickey Cobras and Vice Lords again. *But he's never shown any signs of being involved with a street gang before.*

When I didn't get a call back, I soon drifted to sleep.

I wasn't too worried about Brian. Since his mom had been sentenced to prison for manufacturing drugs, he'd lived with different relatives—for a while with his aunt and his cousins, other

times with his grandmother. He loved to sleep over at the Vranos'
or our house whenever he could finagle an invitation. I was almost
as surprised that his relatives were worried as I was that Brian
hadn't come home. I figured he'd spent the night at some friend's
house without asking permission or bothering to check in. He
would show up in the morning.

When my phone rang again before 7 A.M., I was already in the
shower. My wife, Tina, brought me the cordless.

"Coach Bob?"

"Yes?"

"This is Mrs. Dixon." It was Brian's grandmother this time. But
she was crying, so I couldn't understand everything she said. "It's
... Brian ... the poh-lice say ... hafta 'dentify ... the morgue ..."

Morgue? My body suddenly went numb. *There has to be some
mistake!*

"I'm on my way," I told her.

I hung up, quickly pulled on the suit and tie I'd planned to
wear to my Loop office that morning, and headed for Chicago's
notorious Cabrini-Green neighborhood. Brian's grandmother lived
on the second floor of a run-down three-story walk-up a couple
of blocks from the highrise housing projects. The policemen were
long gone by the time I climbed the steep, darkened stairs to knock
at the Dixon apartment door.

The cops had left the address of the city morgue, where they'd
told Brian's grandma she needed to come to identify his body.

"I'll drive you," I insisted, still hoping there had been some
mistake. It didn't take long to get across town at that hour. Which
seemed like a good thing to me because I had no idea what to say
to the weeping grandmother sitting in my front seat.

I spent the drive thinking about Brian. Images and memories
flashed through my mind.

This was the third season he'd played for the Northwestern Mutual Life Pygmy. Brian wasn't the best baseball player on my team. But he was athletic—one of those unpredictable all or nothing guys who might homer in his first at bat and then strike out every time he came up the rest of the game.

He'd always had a good arm. But his skills had been so raw the first season that except for one failed attempt at pitching, we played him almost exclusively in the outfield. He'd improved enough by the second season that he played most of that year at first base.

I suspected Brian had an attention deficit problem, but a lot of Little Leaguers show those symptoms. One time when he was talking to someone in the dugout, a throw from short hit Brian square in the chest. And I remembered more than a few times seeing him suddenly flinch as our infielders' throws went whistling past his head at first base when he wasn't looking and didn't even know a batter had put the ball in play. Concentration and focus were not Brian's strong suit.

But the image that kept playing through my mind, because it seemed so out of character for such a quiet kid, was the way he always went out to assume his position at the start of every game. Sprinting onto the infield and turning spectacular back flips a la the St. Louis Cardinals' all-star shortstop, Ozzie Smith.

There's gotta be some mistake. Brian was one of those shy, almost withdrawn kids who minded his own business. He didn't mix much with teammates. His place on the bench was always next to Cathy Vranos, Bill's wife, who served as our official scorekeeper and unofficial team mom. No doubt capable of mischief, Brian was a good kid at heart. Eager to please. Willing to try whatever was asked of him. A pleasure to have around. Often came to practice on an old banana-seat bike, painted gold, with no tires. Brian went everywhere riding on the rims. So for his birthday back in December, Coach Bill and I had bought Brian a set of whitewall tires and some new handlebars to really snazz up that old bike. I will never forget the look on his face. He was so proud. And acted so cool.

The morgue's main entrance on Harrison was locked when we arrived. But an attendant, obviously expecting visitors, answered our knock. He signed us in and led us down a hall to a cold, brightly lit room with one entire wall of huge drawers. Walking along the wall, checking the names as he went, the attendant finally stopped and pulled out one of the middle-level drawers.

Fortunately, I had my arm around Mrs. Dixon. Because when the drawer opened enough to reveal Brian's face, she gave out a wrenching cry and her knees buckled. I held her up as the attendant pulled the drawer all the way out.

There lay Brian, wearing his baseball uniform pants, his torso wrapped with white cloth. I could see no injury that looked serious enough to kill anyone, let alone a twelve-year-old kid as full of life as Brian Dixon. My first instinct was to reach out and shake him gently like I do when I wake my own kids in the morning. *Come on, Brian, you need to get up and get moving. You've got a game today.*

Then I noticed the large, dark bloodstain which had soaked through the sheet and pad beneath him. And I realized all the life had drained out of that little body as well.

Looking down at the remains of her young grandson in that body bag, Mrs. Dixon managed merely to nod and sob, "That's him." A disbelieving whisper, "That's my Brian." The drawer slid closed with a solid, metallic *ka-chunk*.

There was no mistake. Brian Dixon was dead. Details were sketchy and contradictory. Senseless murder or tragic accident? Not that it mattered now, but the spruced-up bicycle we'd given him was gone.

Mrs. Dixon signed some papers. Then I drove her home, where she fixed me tea and we talked fondly of Brian until family friends and relatives began to arrive.

Trying to be strong for Brian's grandmother, I'd managed to keep it together all morning. But alone in my car, driving toward the office, the reality of what had happened suddenly hit me. I barely managed to pull my car onto the shoulder of the southbound Kennedy Expressway before I lost it.

I swore and smacked the steering wheel. "God, I've got nothing else to say!" I was angry and hurting. No pious platitudes would cut it. No simple sermon on "God's perfect and precious will" could ever soothe this deep of a wound.

Brian's killing may have been random, vicious insanity. But the pain was personal.

Bam! Bam! Bam! Three times I punched the inside of my windshield. The glass shattered so easily from the inside. I climbed out of the car to survey the damage.

"Great, just great," I fumed.

Then with two hands I furiously twisted and yanked the driver's side mirror off my own car and pitched it onto the side of the road. Breathing hard from that exertion, I suddenly realized I was now crying all over the expressway shoulder, right there in front of all Chicago. People driving past must have wondered what maniac was dismantling his Ford Taurus station wagon on the side of the Kennedy in broad daylight.

Nobody stopped. I stood there all alone. Helpless. Realizing that I had no play. No matter where I threw, it would make no difference for Brian. He would never man first base again.

I eventually got in my car and drove home, negotiating the familiar route through a blur of tears. There in my living room I sank into a chair and rocked my baby son to sleep on my chest. It wasn't even lunchtime, but I was feeling so lost and far behind, so paralyzed, that I wondered if I'd ever catch up again. As if it mattered.

I called an old friend—my spiritual mentor and former pastor in New York. I told B. J. what had gone down and tried to describe just how empty I felt. We prayed for Brian's family. That made me feel a little less hollow.

I confessed that I'd had a fight with my car.

"Who won?" B. J. quipped.

I had to smile. But I hurt way too much to laugh.

MOURNING

My mood didn't improve when I read the newspaper coverage of Brian's death the next day.

I found the article buried on page 3 of the "Chicagoland" section of the *Chicago Tribune* for Thursday, May 13, 1993. The headline read "Youth's 'Tough Life' Comes to Violent End." The article began:

> To most adults, Brian Dixon was trouble, and troubled. A behavior problem and a poor student, the slightly built 7th grader was filled with anger, those who knew him said.
>
> On Tuesday night, a bullet from a Smith & Wesson .357 revolver ripped into his back, severed his spine, punctured his windpipe and cut a major artery before it left his chest just above the heart. He was dead in minutes.
>
> Brian Dixon was 13. [He] ... lived much of his life in the Cabrini-Green public housing development on the Near North Side, but two years ago he moved to Humboldt Park with his mother and brother.
>
> Last year he and his brother moved in with an aunt, Antoinette Dixon, after his mother was sentenced to prison....
>
> "I worked with him and got to know him pretty well," said Von Humboldt [school] Assistant Principal Chris Kalamatas.

"He was in trouble a lot. He never was arrested; he was just disruptive.

"He had a very tough life.... He spent a lot of time on the streets ... for a 13-year-old." ...

"We see children like Brian; they come to school with anger in them," Kalamatas said. "He was always wonderful with me, but I can't say that for others. He defied authority."

Four months earlier, in January of 1993, the *Chicago Tribune* had run a series titled "Killing Our Children," which chronicled the story of every child in our city under the age of fifteen who had died a violent death during the previous year. Sixty-two children in all. In the follow-up series of editorials on children and violence, which earned the *Trib* a Pulitzer Prize, the paper said, "The increasing proliferation of handgun violence in Chicago and across the U.S. is a national disgrace. The toll in deaths and shattered lives, particularly on our children, has reached staggering numbers."

Neither journalistic concern nor public outcry made any difference to Brian Dixon. Four months after the paper's award-winning series on children and violence, he was just another victim whose death warranted no more than a single article, a story with a headline and content which caricatured a "troubled" youth whose "violent end" was made to seem a sadly inevitable, almost fitting, culmination of his "tough life."

I barely recognized the boy in that newspaper article—the description just didn't fit. I never once thought of Brian as "tough." And he certainly didn't defy the authority of his Little League coaches.

On the contrary, his craving of our time and attention was so transparent we had to laugh about it—the way he always schemed to be the last one delivered home so he could have one-on-one time in the car with me or with Bill. And the times he'd call the house just to say hello and ask what we were doing, obviously hoping for an invitation to come over.

Brian seemed to genuinely enjoy my children, volunteering to carry one of them whenever he went somewhere with us. He would tease and tickle and play with our toddlers like a big brother. Then he would gently tuck blankets around them when they fell asleep in their car seats.

As soon as Bill Vranos learned of Brian's death, he called his wife. Cathy cut her business trip short and caught the first flight back to Chicago. Both she and Bill were devastated. They'd really gotten attached and had spent a lot more time with Brian than I had. They too knew the newspaper article had not even begun to tell the whole story.

Bill and Cathy Vranos were typical of the volunteers we recruited to get involved in the Little League I'd helped found— busy professionals who made a serious commitment of time and energy, not to mention money. Bill's grueling residency program kept him on duty ninety to a hundred hours or more every week. Cathy put in fifty- to sixty-hour weeks for Chicago's Leo Burnett Advertising Agency. What little spare time they did have they devoted to the league and the kids—not just during baseball season but all year round.

The Vranoses both seemed to have a special attachment to Brian from the beginning. He may have even had something of a crush on Cathy. He always loved visiting their home and romping around the park chasing their golden retriever, Duke.

The Brian we saw on the field was quiet and shy around his teammates. But never too shy to call us up and invite himself over. One time he phoned Bill and Cathy on Christmas Day to ask what they were doing. When it dawned on them that his family didn't have any special Christmas plans, they drove over and picked

Brian up so he could celebrate the rest of the holiday with them. Bill is a big sports fan, so one of the fun things Cathy had done was give him a bunch of baseball cards. So the Vranoses wrapped those back up and made a big production of giving them to Brian.

Brian talked about his family a lot. The first year or so on our team, he was always wanting Bill and Cathy to meet his mom. When they'd drop him off at his apartment, he'd ask them to "wait just a minute. My mama say she come meet you today." He'd be back a minute or two later, his head hanging, apologetic. "She be busy right now."

"That's okay," Cathy would reassure him. "We'll meet your mother next time." But they never did.

In addition to his family, Brian talked about the shootings he'd heard and seen. He tried so hard to be matter-of-fact about it, like it didn't bother him at all. But one day he relaxed his guard just enough to tell Bill and Cathy one of the reasons he loved coming to their house so much. "There be no shootin' 'round here."

Brian visited the Vranos' home so often that the landlord of their Lincoln Park apartment building complained to them that "he scares some of the other tenants." I remember Bill being furious when he told me about that, because we both knew the landlord wouldn't have ever said a word if Brian had been white.

When the Vranos' lease came up for renewal, the landlord really jacked up the rent. But Bill and Cathy had already found another place, primarily because of the man's attitude toward Brian. They cared about their relationship with him that much.

So when several days passed and the Dixon family couldn't tell us about their funeral plans, Cathy called Johnson's Funeral Home up on North Avenue to inquire about the delay. "We don't have Brian Dixon's body yet," she was told. "He's still at the morgue."

When she demanded to know why, she was told that the family had yet to pay for the services of the funeral home—nine hundred dollars (in advance) for everything: embalming, the casket, a wake and memorial service, plus interment in a local cemetery. The funeral director was almost apologetic. But he explained to Cathy he had done business in the neighborhood for years; he could no longer afford to provide services he might never get paid for.

Cathy was so appalled that Brian's body remained in the morgue with no prospect of a proper burial that she instructed the funeral director to get the body, saying she would guarantee payment. Then Cathy came to me so upset we immediately agreed to share the cost.

The next day, I received a phone call. Another snag. The funeral director told me the family had learned the only way Lawanda Dixon, Brian's mom, would be allowed to attend the funeral was if someone paid for her transportation from prison and for accompanying security. "The family says they don't have the money to do that," the man told me.

"How much?" I wanted to know.

"Four hundred dollars," he said.

I couldn't believe it.

"The state requires that two armed guards travel with all prisoners," he explained. I checked and the man was telling the truth. Two armed guards would cost four hundred dollars.

It looked as if the only way Brian's mom would be able to say goodbye to her dead son was if we paid for it. So we wrote another check. But it all seemed so insane!

Brian's grandma seemed very appreciative. She also asked if I would speak at the service. I said I would. Which meant I spent a lot of time over the next couple of days thinking about Brian and trying to decide what I was going to say.

So many memories came to mind. One of my favorites took place during a game. I don't remember who we were playing, but as was often the case, we had two games going simultaneously on opposite corners of our field. We had no home-run fences, and the dimensions were short enough that sometimes the outfielders in the two games actually overlapped. For safety purposes—since they couldn't watch both directions at once—we sometimes equipped outfielders with batting helmets so they wouldn't get conked on the head from behind.

On this particular occasion, I heard the crack of the bat on the far diamond. A deep drive to center sailed past both center fielders and bounded onto our infield. Our umpire called time and everyone in our game stopped to watch the action.

In the distance, an extremely large slugger, enormous for a twelve-year-old, lumbered around first base like he was running in slow-motion replay. The speedy center fielder was already retrieving the ball way over on our pitcher's mound. Most players in our league would be crossing home plate and accepting high fives on the way to the dugout by now, but this Fat Albert prototype was just barely chugging through second base as the center fielder cut loose a long throw to his left fielder, who was now in our outfield waiting for the relay.

Our game remained on hold. Everyone on our field—players, coaches, umpires, and spectators—had turned to watch. All eyes were on the big boy, uniform bulging, now huffing and puffing around the base path.

Brian Dixon was rolling on the infield grass, hysterical with laughter. "Ol' boy be slooo-oow!"

The players were merciless. My whole team was now laughing and pointing. "Look at 'im, look at 'im!"

The left fielder took the relay, pivoted, and threw. The straining and staggering runner stumble-slid in a cloud of dust. He was out—by five feet—at third.

Now several of my players, following Brian's lead, were rolling in the grass hysterical. Both dugouts on our field emptied. Everyone was laughing and mimicking the runner in the distance, who was now arguing the call.

"Hey!" I laughingly shouted at Brian. "Come on, dude, don't be so-o mean! Can we finish *our* game now?"

But he wasn't actually being mean. All the boys (and a lot of adults) had been laughing. It was a pretty comical scene. And the laughter it inspired was more spontaneous and innocent than it was calculated and cruel. Brian wasn't really mean, any more than he was tough.

Most of the kids in our Little League program who had spent their whole lives in the projects were very streetwise. Yet they had little or no experience outside their own neighborhood. They lived within five or six city blocks of Chicago's magnificent lakeshore parks, and yet some of them had never even seen Lake Michigan.

So I would take a whole carload of boys to the lake for a swim after practice on hot summer days. I also tried to give my players some cross-cultural experience by taking them on road trips to play friendly scrimmages against teams from suburban and rural downstate baseball leagues. And after the end of our first season, I'd started what would become an annual tradition by taking my entire Pygmy team on a barnstorming tour to Iowa, which may not seem like heaven to city kids but is definitely a very strange and exciting place for those who have never seen live cows or cornfields before.

We camped out in Iowa, another first for most of our players. And in time-honored camping tradition, we sat around a blazing fire each night telling scary stories. Even normal night sounds of the forest alarmed our city kids, who'd never heard crickets and owls before. So they were petrified when we recounted horror tales about the dreaded Iowa hillbillies who lived in the surrounding woods and sometimes kidnapped unsuspecting campers who wandered too far from the fire at night.

The boys laughed off the stories with the predictable bravado of young boys everywhere. Some nights when I'd tell them to quiet down and go to sleep, they'd still be lyin' under their blankets bragging about what they would do if "some ol' hillbilly try to snatch me; he be real sorry!"

But invariably we coaches would wake up the next morning amused to find little bodies crammed in tightly around us. It seemed every boy had a hand reaching out, gripping the edge of a coach's sleeping bag, searching for some comfort and the reassurance of adult contact. Brian was almost always wedged up next to Bill Vranos, one arm draped over Bill's dog, Duke.

So much for the tough guys.

But perhaps my all-time favorite memory of Brian is another Iowa experience. One of our hosts for those trips was a doctor friend in Dubuque who volunteered to take all our players for a ride in his single-engine plane. For kids who had never been in an airplane before, those flights were the highlight of the trip. Literally and figuratively.

Of course, since the plane was small, the boys had to wait patiently and take turns going up. But somehow Brian managed to scheme his way into the plane for a second flight. I called him on it when he got back down and I realized what had happened. But I couldn't be very upset with him when I saw the look of absolute joy and wonder on his face. I'll never forget it.

Brian's wake and memorial service finally took place on May 19, eight days after he was killed. Family and friends gathered in a small and rather dingy viewing room on the second floor of the North Avenue storefront funeral home. His grandmother had requested he be buried in his Little League uniform.

I had thought the saddest thing I'd ever seen was Brian's body lying lifeless in the morgue. That was before I saw Brian's mother, Lawanda Dixon, being escorted into the funeral home that afternoon in handcuffs. Her guards allowed her to walk up to the casket by herself, but as she stood for a time at her little boy's side, whenever she reached down to touch him or reached up to brush a tear out of her eye, she had to do it with both hands still cuffed.

Then she couldn't even stay for the service. Her guards had to have her back at the prison that afternoon.

Our entire Pygmy team showed up in uniform for the visitation time prior to the service. The program actually listed the team, and me as Brian's coach, among his survivors. I walked with the other boys up to the casket, and they all hung around as I introduced myself to some of the relatives.

Brian's dad was there. I'd never met the man, but I'd have recognized him anywhere because Brian looked just like him. He looked fifteen, maybe twenty, years older than Brian's mom. I had no idea how long they'd been divorced, or if they'd ever been married, since his last name was not Dixon.

A few minutes before the service was scheduled to start, I noticed the people around me looking toward the door in the back of the room. Then the crowd slowly parted as Brian's eighteen- or nineteen-year-old brother, Calvin, sauntered in followed by a long line of gang members.

Each of them had on a T-shirt on which they had hand-lettered "RIP Little Bri." They filed through the other mourners and assumed positions in a semicircle around Brian's casket. There, with their backs turned so the rest of us couldn't see exactly what they were doing, the GDs went through a series of hand gestures, evidently some kind of private ritual. Then they stood in silence for a few moments before retreating, in single file again, to the back of the room.

Bill Vranos told me later that their little ceremonial thing made him so angry he could barely contain himself. He said it was all he could do not to scream and order the gangbangers to get out, that if anyone was to blame for Brian's death, it was them, with their gang culture marked by violence, drugs, and guns.

I'd been around long enough to see beyond the obvious. I knew these kids felt isolated, were afraid of being laughed at, and may have gotten involved in gangs just because they wanted to be part of something. But when I looked at those kids, I couldn't help thinking of what my friend Sam Dillon had told me. Sam was in his fifties and had been a leader years earlier for the notorious Blackstone Rangers. He had recently completed a long prison sentence for killing two people in a fight. A very bright guy who had really turned his life around, Sam often spoke contemptuously of today's gangs. He'd said, "In the old days, you had to be strong to be a gang leader. Because we fought one another with our fists— and sometimes with knives. You didn't last long in the gangs unless you was really tough. But no one has to be tough today. Any scrawny little punk carryin' a 9 millimeter automatic could blow away Mike Tyson. But take away they firepower and they nothin', man. They pathetic, really."

I didn't see any weapons in the funeral home that evening. And I had to agree with Sam's assessment. To me the gangbangers looked more pathetic than tough.

The service started and almost before I realized it, it was my turn to speak. I walked to the front and stood behind a little podium facing the small crowd that had gathered. I couldn't help contrasting the row of young boys in their Pygmy baseball uniforms sitting down front with the older gang guys in the back wearing their hand-lettered tribute to "Little Bri."

I don't remember much of what I said. I do know I started by looking right at Brian's brother and his fellow gang members and saying, "It's time to take your hats off, fellas." And they did.

I kept it brief. Got a little choked up when I told about Brian flying in that plane in Iowa. What a thrill that was for him. How excited he'd been to go up in the clouds and look down at everything below. Then I said something about knowing Brian was up in heaven now, looking down again at all of us from a better place.

In all I probably spoke for about five minutes. I remember quoting what Malcolm X said in refusing to use armed bodyguards after someone burned his home. Just before he was murdered, Malcolm brushed off concern for his own welfare and said, "If I can't be safe among my own kind, where can I be?"

And I remember telling my team and the GDs, "The deck has been stacked against you. And it's still stacked against you." Then I ended by pounding on the podium and looking right at those young men to plead, "We've got to stop this! We've got to stop killing each other!"

Driving home afterward, I wondered, *What more should I have said?* As if it could have made any difference.

The senselessness and the futility overwhelmed me.

What if we hadn't fixed up Brian's bike? What if he had been with me the night he was killed? He should have been with me that night! Why didn't we find a way to move Brian to our street, like we did with another player's family?

What more could I have said or done that would have helped? Why did I ever think a Little League program might make a difference? What in the world am I doing here anyway?

The truth was I knew some amazingly positive relationships were nurtured through our baseball program. Volunteers stuck around to mentor and tutor kids in the off-season. Many coaches raised and donated funds to pay tuition for some of their players to enroll in parochial and private schools. Players and sometimes their family members were now working for men and and women they would never have met if not for the league.

But no one said it would be easy. And it hasn't been easy from day one.

The first year of our league, few of the kids had ever played an organized sport before. So I thought it might be both instructive and inspirational to take Brian and the other boys to a major league baseball game. The Oakland A's just happened to be in town playing the Chicago White Sox the night before our league's opening day.

"You can all wear your uniforms to the game," I told the kids. "It'll be great to see how baseball is supposed to be played just before we start our season."

And it was a memorable experience for all concerned. I don't think any of our boys had ever been to a big league ballpark. Most of them, like Brian, spent the entire evening mouths-agape and wide-eyed with amazement as they took in the wonder of the new Comiskey Park, the huge crowd, and the biggest, brightest, lushest field of green grass any of them had ever seen. We bought programs, and I tried to teach some of them the rudiments of scorekeeping. But I spent the better part of the game constantly encouraging my young charges to watch the action on the field so they could learn how baseball was played by real pros.

Unfortunately, I nearly choked on those words when Jose Canseco exchanged threats with the pitcher after being hit by a pitch. A few pitches later, his hard slide into second base triggered a bench-clearing brawl that delayed the game for several minutes and resulted in a variety of expulsions and fines. *Great job, gentlemen.*

"Look at that, Coach," one of the kids exclaimed. "We gonna kick some butt tomorrow!" We'd obviously have to look for better behavioral examples and have a talk about sportsmanship later.

Predictably, the fight seemed, if not the most popular, at least the loudest topic of conversation on the ride home after the game. I cringed to hear more than one player threaten what he would do if anyone ever hit him with a pitch.

I flinched again minutes later, but for a very different reason, when I felt two thumps in the back of my car as we waited for a red light in front of the Castle, one of the largest and most ominous of all the Cabrini-Green buildings. It felt like someone had smacked the rear of my station wagon with a baseball bat, twice. Then an angry black face appeared just inches from mine and a fist hammered my driver's side window.

"You lost? You a tourist? Whatchu doin' here?"

"Hey, man!" I yelled back. "I'm a baseball coach and I'm just taking my players home." When I jerked my thumb over my shoulder, I saw the guy's eyes shift to take in my carload of uniforms and black faces.

His expression changed. "Sorry, Coach!" he said and waved me on.

It wasn't until I'd dropped off the last of the players and pulled into my garage ten minutes later that I got out and walked around my station wagon to discover both taillights had been shattered. I didn't learn what had happened until I took it to the shop for repairs. My mechanic found two bullet holes, one on each side. If whoever shot out my taillights had aimed just a few inches higher, somebody inside that station wagon might have died.

That was my very first year with the league. I really should have known then what I was getting into.

Brian easily could have died that night. Two years earlier.

I thanked God he hadn't. Otherwise I never would have really known him.

Nor would I have felt such pain at his loss.

RUN

It's almost dawn.

I descend the front steps of my house and head north on Oakley. Like I do every morning that I run in to work, I turn left on Harrison and begin my trek heading west, away from my downtown office.

Our West Side neighborhood is part of the Harrison district, which had the dubious distinction of leading Chicago in murders again last year. But each new day dawns fresh, peaceful, and promising—even here.

Everything remains steel gray and still as I cross Western Avenue. I can hear the familiar whine of tractor-trailers and the steady hum of tires from the first wave of commuters already on the Eisenhower Expressway just two blocks away.

Chicago rush hour starts early. Everybody in the financial markets here does business on East Coast time.

New York rush hour is later on both ends. Hey, when I lived there, I often didn't make it home until 6 A.M.

Actually, New York City is a great place to be *from*. Everything seems a little easier, a little slower, once you cross the Hudson. Those of us who hail from New York are careful not to speak too fondly of Chicago when we return home visiting or on business. We're afraid they might make us move back east. Or worse yet, more New Yorkers will come out here. Then we'll all be honkin' our horns and talkin' too fast.

I still love NY, but life moves fast enough as it is.

Seven years have passed since Brian's death. Yet I think of him this morning. Because the carnage continues in Chicago, where violence claimed another innocent young victim yesterday.

I never coached twelve-year-old Miguel DeLaRosa, but I knew who he was. He played for the Orioles, another team in our Little League. And he attended the same church I do in Humboldt Park on Chicago's Northwest Side.

One of the coaches called me last evening as soon as he heard the news. The papers carried the story this morning.

On page 3 of the morning's *Chicago Tribune* "Metro" section, the headline announced, "Twelve-Year-Old Fatally Shot in Drive-By."

A 12-year-old boy riding a bike near a Northwest Side street corner was killed Wednesday by shots fired from two passing cars.

Police were seeking the occupants of two vehicles, a van and a sedan, in connection with the shooting, but it was unclear late Wednesday how many people were in the vehicles.

Initial police reports said rival gang members shot at each other from separate cars. But witnesses said they were from the same gang and simply fired shots from the cars as they drove through rival turf.

The boy, Miguel DeLaRosa, was struck at least once in the chest and was pronounced dead at 6:29 p.m. in Children's Memorial Hospital, according to police....

The boy's 11-year-old brother, Angel Lopez, was playing across the street when the shots were fired. He saw his brother fall from the bicycle and then return to his feet.

He yelled several times before collapsing. "His final words were 'They shot me,'" Angel said.

The boy's friends and family gathered later Wednesday at his home in the 4400 block of West Dickens Avenue and remembered Miguel, a 6th grader at Northwest Middle School, as a "comedian" who loved to make people laugh.

A later edition of the paper carried a front-page story under the headline "Killings Spur Call to Action in Humboldt Park Area." That story, telling of a mother's heartbreak, began:

As she did every Wednesday, Natividad Lopez began to worry as soon as she dropped off her 12-year-old son, Miguel DeLaRosa, in their old Northwest Side neighborhood for Bible study and baseball.

A year ago, driven by violence and gangs, the family had moved out of the tense area just north and east of Humboldt Park, and she felt as if little had changed. Gunfire still crackled through summer nights. The streets still roared with screeching tires.

This week Lopez's worst fears came true as Miguel was shot in the chest and killed, knocked off a friend's bicycle after a baseball game. He was an innocent victim caught in the cross-fire between rival gangs, police said.

Violence devastates so many families who have had kids in our baseball program. Yet we've never had any of our players or coaches seriously injured on our fields. Which is just one reason I believe in prayer. It's also why I make it habit when I go to my office in the mornings to first head west for five blocks, away from downtown, so I can pray as I run around our Altgeld Park baseball diamonds, thanking God for, and asking protection over, all that goes on there. I find that morning ritual invigorating. And I'm in special need of such encouragement this morning.

I splash through a puddle under the viaduct over Harrison. There are always puddles down there, even if it doesn't rain. It's the worst spot on my entire route. You're really taking your chances running under here in the evening, when this place is a gauntlet. Mike Clark, one of our best volunteer coaches, was pelted with rocks earlier in the season beneath this viaduct.

Wrong guy. Though he's going on forty, Mike is still faster than most kids. But when he started to chase the perpetrators, they sprinted over the footbridge spanning the Eisenhower Expressway. Mike was gaining on them as they crossed into the Rockwell Gardens projects. *Now what, Mikey? What are you gonna do if you catch four teenagers on a Friday night in one of the roughest housing projects on the entire West Side?*

Yeah right! Mike jogged back to Altgeld Park and coached his game. Sometimes it's like when the lion in *The Wizard of Oz* reads the sign "Haunted Forest. I'd turn back if I were you."

In my neighborhood you gotta learn when to turn back. *But hey, walk away, live to coach another day.*

Today is another day. The sky brightens behind me, the sidewalk rises in front of me. As I emerge from the tunnel, on my right are three manicured ball diamonds with dugouts, lights, and everything. Altgeld Park has become a shining green emerald in a rough part of our neighborhood. It's the place suburban commuters see—lit up like Wrigley Field—on the south side of the Ike as they journey home to the promised land each night.

Before we got the lights installed, we had to make a point of showing up early for Saturday morning games in order to collect the used needles and condoms out of our dugouts. Since our lights were installed, the hookers and the junkies have taken their activities elsewhere. And the neighborhood has gladly traded the darkness for the familiar summer sounds of the crack of the bat, the laughter of children, and the roar of umpires shouting "Play ball!"

Well, most people see it as an improvement anyway. I can't help chuckling whenever I remember the complaint of a former Chicago Parks District supervisor who once staffed the Altgeld field house. "This was a nice, quiet little park until you and your Little League started here!" she told me one day.

"That's fine, ma'am, " I told her. "But this is a park. It shouldn't be quiet. It needs to be used by the community. In fact, this place ought to be rockin'!"

And now it does rock. Five nights a week and all day Saturday, from May through Labor Day, the largest inner-city Little League program in America plays here, with two, sometimes three, games going at a time on this Chicago field of dreams.

Despite the sadness I feel this morning, just looking out over the green grass of our diamonds triggers so many warm memories I have to smile to myself as I run along the center field fence. My smile widens as I spot the daily homeless parade coming toward me on the sidewalk ahead.

Three hundred and sixty-five nights a year, a Franciscan mission at Harrison and Washtenaw (just across the street from Altgeld Park) sleeps about a hundred needy men. And a few women too. After a warm, crowded night's sleep, the priests offer their guests a bite to eat and it's time to go. That's when the morning march eastward begins.

On cold winter days, many of these poor souls wrap garbage bags around their feet to try to stay dry and warm. They may be able to stop for a few minutes to rest in the comfort of the ER waiting room at Cook County Hospital a dozen blocks away. But they aren't usually welcome there for long before they must begin the second half of their hike downtown. Many spend their days in and around Pacific Garden Mission on State Street just south of the Loop. Others will panhandle and look for familiar downtown haunts to stand or sit out of the wind and weather.

On such a nice warm summer morning as this, no one is hurrying. So I slow to a walk in order to better greet some of the finest Little League fans I've ever seen anywhere. Many of these guys rarely miss an evening game because they gather at Altgeld Park to wait for the shelter doors to open for the night. They enthusiastically cheer the kids without ever chewing out an umpire or insisting that a coach "put my son in!"

Sometimes one or more of them will be obviously intoxicated, but they rarely cause any problems to speak of.

There are rare exceptions. One time a pathetic old codger staggered into right field during one of our games, dropped his trousers in full sight of everyone, and actually defecated in the grass. He was truly lost.

The players all thought the scene hilarious—except, of course, the right fielders on both teams. I didn't know whether to laugh or cry as I helped the poor guy pull up his pants, put my arm over his shoulders, and guided him slowly back through the fence to the sidewalk.

I don't see that man walking toward me this morning. But there are lots of other familiar faces.

"Hey buddy, ya gotta smoke?" asks a middle-aged bald guy wearing two pairs of pants and a T-shirt.

"No man, I don't have to smoke," I joke back.

"Hey Coach Bob. How ya doin'?" It's Freddie. He umpires the bases for us sometimes on nights when he's not disabled. He really knows and loves baseball.

"G'morning, Fred," I respond.

"Looks like rain. Think you'll play tonight, Coach?"

"I wish it would rain beer!" the smoker rasps between hacking coughs before I can respond.

"No, I weesh it would rain tequila," pipes up a small man with a big moustache and a distinctly Mexican accent. I grin at this reminder that with a decent night's sleep, even an active alcoholic can find reason for hope and optimism in the morning.

The little fellow is still a strikingly handsome man, which amazes me, because I know from experience the beating he must have given himself over the years to end up here. He begins a slow, circular two-step while pretending to play a horn with his fingers in front of his mouth. The guy does a pretty good trumpet imitation.

As he starts dancing to the familiar trumpet tune of that old one-word song, he pulls a pint bottle out of his back pocket. There's one tiny swig left in the bottom. *The last hit was always the saddest one.*

Da-dunt data dunta-dunta. Da-da data dunta da. The mock musician raises his trumpet with a great flourish and shouts the one-word lyric that inspires his hope and no doubt reminded him of this tune.

"Te-quil-a."

With that he leans his head back and drains the last drop from his bottle.

A few men, heavy laden with garbage bags full of all they've got, have stopped and blocked the sidewalk to watch the trumpeteer. Now they begin to move again as the morning parade slowly marches east.

Waving my goodbyes, I pass through a gap in the fence and cut across one of our ball diamonds. Standing at a water fountain on the other side of the park is just the man I'd hoped to see.

"Hey Miles!" I call as I begin to run toward him. Miles Blackman is the Near West Little League's most faithful umpire and a longtime friend who lives off and on with various relatives around the neighborhood and sometimes sleeps in my basement. He evidently spent last night in the shelter.

"Hi, Bob," Miles greets me as I pull to a halt in front of him. "You runnin' t' work?"

"Yep. Headin' downtown," I tell him. "But I was hopin' I'd see you this morning to let you know tonight's games have all been canceled."

"No . . . no game tonight?" Miles is obviously disappointed. I knew he would be. He really looks forward to baseball season, when he can umpire six days a week. "Why no game? How come?" he wants to know.

"One of our players was shot and killed up in Humboldt Park yesterday," I say. I explain what had happened and how we had decided to cancel all of tonight's games in Miguel's honor.

"Okay," Miles says, resignedly. "Guess I'll see you tomorrow?"

"How about tonight? There's gonna be a memorial service for Miguel. I can pick you up here at six."

Miles grins and nods. "Okay!"

"Okay!" I respond. "I'll see ya then, buddy. I've gotta go now."

"You gotta run to work?"

"All the way," I say.

He grins and shakes his head as he watches me take off.

I'm running along the north side of Altgeld Park now with the Eisenhower on my left, finally heading toward downtown. Three miles in front of me, the Sears Tower dominates Chicago's skyline and seems to grow taller as I run toward it.

Occasionally a billboard blocks my view of the city at sunrise. I grimace as I approach one of the dozens of Martel Cognac signs "strategically placed" in our neighborhood. Whoever designed that company's marketing campaign ought to get fired. Like most of the others, this billboard features a handsome African-American couple dressed in evening gown and tux, sipping from a glass of Martel, I guess.

But wait! What's that? At the foot of the steel pole holding up the billboard, a pile of rags begins to move. A glassy-eyed man sits up. His Rastafarian dreadlocks are matted with vomit. *What happened? Was it the Martel?* He might have started out that way. But the cheap Thunderbird wine chaser is where he ended up. The poor fellow opens his eyes wide, threatens the sky, and pukes again.

My morning run continues. I'm thankful as always to be running to work at this hour and not just coming in from the night before. Lest I forget, that could have been me under the billboard.

I catch a glimpse of the sun peeking around the edge of the John Hancock Building. I pick up my pace, closing in on the city. One of the reasons I run to work in the mornings is to pray and have some personal quiet time. But today the "hymn" I can't quit humming in my head is "Da-da dada dunta da! Tequila!"

Downtown, after showering and getting dressed at the LaSalle Club, I settle into my tenth-floor corner office overlooking the busy intersection of Madison and Franklin. I spend my working hours as the president of my own small insurance-brokerage firm, Benefit Planning, Inc. We tax-leverage insurance products, representing any number of companies but primarily working with the Northwestern Mutual Financial Network.

Most of our clients are players in the financial markets either in Chicago or New York—working on the Mercantile Exchange, the Board of Trade, the New York Stock Exchange—buying and selling stock, bonds, or commodities futures for themselves and their clients. Or they work for Wall Street and LaSalle Street firms that do.

I've found that a lot of very successful people who do a great job of looking out for the financial interests of their clients often don't have time to do the same for themselves, their families, and their employees. So that's the niche we try to fill.

I guess that means my official profession would be listed as business executive. But most of the time, especially in the spring and summer, when someone asks me what I do, my instinctive reaction, my first thought, is likely to be, "I coach Little League baseball."

For the past ten years, I've coached in and been either president or vice president of four city Little Leagues. My wife, Tina, and I cofounded these leagues with various friends almost as crazy as we were. I say crazy because these are not typical Little Leagues, and when we started doing this, most of us didn't even have kids, or at least not kids of playing age.

Why'd we do it? For my part, I can say it was because I loved God, kids, and baseball. I wanted to be a good neighbor. And I was just trying to do the next right thing.

After all, somebody coached me when I was growing up.

THE KING AND I

The name is Muzikowski. But I grew up Irish Catholic.

My grandmother, Mary Walsh, came over on the boat from County Down, Ireland, as a teenager about the turn of the last century. Soon after her arrival, she married my grandfather. She gave birth to six children and buried three of them—one died in a playground accident, another from tuberculosis, and a third "from the drink." She lived the last eighty years of her life in Brooklyn, then Bayonne, New Jersey—never more than a few miles from where she and so many millions of other poor immigrants landed at Ellis Island.

After being widowed, Nana lived in an apartment either upstairs or downstairs from my mother, from a time before I was born until she died at the age of ninety-six. She always claimed it was a shot of good Irish whiskey a day that preserved her. Though she once admitted to me that her secret to longevity "didn'a work s' good for everone else, ye see thet now."

Grandpa Walsh worked for J and L Steel and brewed his own beer all through Prohibition, my mother's formative years. Mom recalls times when something went amiss with the basement distilling process and the whole family could hear the corks popping all the way upstairs. Then Grandpa would come stomping and swearing up the cellar steps knowing he'd "hafta go down to the guineas with nothing to trade" to his Italian friends for the wine they made in their cellars.

A few months after her father's death, my mother married "that Polack," which is how her family referred to my father. "We broke the block," my mother always said of their intermarriage. It wasn't until later, when I was growing up, that the same term would be applied to the first "turncoat" in the neighborhood to sell his home to a black family. *What? Did'n'cha know thet now?*

My older brother was born nine months and three days after my parents' wedding. According to my mother, all the old biddies in the neighborhood had their calendars out doing the math on that one.

A couple of years later, in the spring of 1956, Dr. Morris Shapiro smacked Mary Walsh's next grandson the minute I arrived in this world. Like a lot of city kids, I kept on getting smacked around after that.

Our family's surname came to us from my paternal grandfather, Joseph Muzikowski, a Polish immigrant whose service in the United States Army's 79th Infantry Division during World War I earned him his citizenship. But as proud as "Pop" was to be an American, his heart remained Polish.

Following one of his many physical encounters with the Bayonne Police Department, it was strongly suggested that my grandfather "go back where he came from." Which he did in the spring of 1939.

Bad timing.

Since Pop had experience in the last big fight, he was soon conscripted into the Polish cavalry. Middle-aged Polish men on horseback, no matter how courageous, weren't much of a match for

Hitler's awesome blitzkrieg. In August of '39, my grandfather lost both his horse and his right leg in a battle between his cavalry unit and Nazi tanks. Grandpa survived somehow. But he was forced to endure the remainder of the war in German-occupied Poland, unable to return home to his family in New Jersey until 1946.

My dad and his two brothers all signed up for military service the day after Pearl Harbor. Uncle Joe, who would later become my godfather, joined the army air corps and served throughout the war as a bombardier and photographer on low-flying reconnaissance planes in the South Pacific. Uncle Lenny joined the army and then re-upped with the navy after the war to pursue a military career. My father, Edward, served in the army engineer corps, helping supply and equip the troops landing in Italy and France.

I sometimes overheard conversations sitting around at family picnics or in bars about "bodies floatin' in the water like so many logs" and "flack so thick you couldn't see nuthin'." But that was among themselves. My father and his brothers, like most men in what has been aptly dubbed "the greatest generation," never felt the need to talk to others much about their accomplishments. Or about their feelings.

The biggest concession to sentiment I ever saw from them was the way they would always stand at attention with hands over their hearts, teary eyed during the playing of the national anthem. They all knew what freedom cost, and it meant something to them.

As a child, my interaction with the men in my family or neighborhood was usually limited to Friday nights and Saturdays. Once I reached the age of about six and was considered "old enough to carry," they'd send me around the corner to Duffy's Tavern to get them fifty-cent pitchers of beer. I remember sipping the suds and wondering why anyone would ever want to drink such awful-tasting stuff. But I was always glad to fetch a pitcher or three in return for the nickel or dime tip one of them usually slipped me for candy.

Grandpa Muzikowski might have been the toughest old dog in the pack. Almost every day, rather than pay the fifteen-cent Broadway bus fare, Pop would hike the twenty-three blocks to our house on Forty-sixth from the Twenty-third Street YMCA where he lived the last fifteen years of his life. Sometimes he wore a wooden prosthesis, but more often than not he'd arrive on crutches, his empty pant leg flappin' in the breeze, maybe carryin' a ten-pound log of bologna tucked under a bicep that would have made Charles Atlas proud. "Found this along the way," he'd say, handing Mom the hunk of meat. "Musta fallen off a truck or somethin'."

Everyone would chuckle. But whenever the Westinghouse plant went on strike, the welcome assortment of goods that "fell off a truck" really saved us.

Dad's job was to work hard every day at the factory. I don't think he was late to work a day in his life.

My mother's job was to take care of the house, the kids, and Dad. Loretta Muzikowski (Lulu to family and close friends) was the chief dispenser of affection and discipline for me and my siblings. And when it came to toughness, the men in the family had nothing over her. Mom had the lookaway move down better than Magic Johnson. She could stare at my brother Jack on her right and *(smack)* nail me with a solid left to my ear. She demanded respect and made sure we gave it. As for our moral, spiritual, and educational development, she left all of that to the good sisters of the Order of St. Joseph and the Holy Catholic Church.

In Bayonne, when anyone asked where you lived, you never said "on the Boulevard and Fifty-sixth near the Jersey City line" or "West Forty-sixth Street," where we moved about the time I started school. What you answered, what people really wanted to know, was the name of your parish: "We live in St. Vinnie's."

Bayonne was only about ten blocks wide, from the Newark Bay side of our narrow peninsula over to the New York Harbor on the east. St. Vincent's, our Irish parish, ran from the city line at Fifty-seventh all the way to Fortieth Street. St. Andrew's, St. Henry's, and Our Lady Star of the Sea were also predominantly Irish. Assumption was the Italian parish. Mount Carmel Parish, down in the twenties where my grandfather lived, was Polish.

Our family never ate meat on Fridays. My mother always quit drinking during Lent.

The church calendar, with its celebration of all of our faith's greatest holy days—Christmas, Easter, All Saints' Day, All Souls, the Immaculate Conception, and the Assumption—served to dominate and divide up the year. But by the age of seven, I discovered New York Yankees baseball, and I never viewed the seasons of the year the same again.

August was sweltering in 1963. Nobody we knew had air conditioning yet, so you had to go outside and find a breeze. The stoops were full those summer nights. Children played under the streetlights long after dark until they heard their father's shrill whistle. Or until someone called their name.

One humid, sticky Friday night after dinner, my dad headed around the corner to Duffy's Tavern. Payday. Time to shoot the breeze, watch the ballgame, and down a couple of cold ones after a hard week's work.

He handed me a dollar bill to fetch him two packs of Chesterfield Kings down at O'Donnel's Sweet Shop with instructions to "meet me at Duffy's in ten minutes."

"Okay," I said.

"Hey."

"What?"

"Keep the change."

I grinned from ear to ear. My father's daily two-pack ration of cigarettes cost only seventy cents. With the thirty cents left for me, I could buy some serious candy. On top of that, Duffy's Tavern had ceiling fans, rotary fans, and best of all, baseball fans. Which meant the Yankee game would be on TV.

As I expected, Red Duffy, owner, bartender, chief cook and bottle washer, set me up with my own place at the bar when I arrived. "Hey, it's Muzzy's kid. Howsa 'bout a coke and a Slim Jim?"

I climbed on my stool, strategically located directly in front of the television set high above the bar. The place smelled like one great big giant cigar encrusted with stale beer and sawdust. The doors were wide open, so the enticing noise and odor spilled out onto Forty-seventh Street.

The tavern had been more crowded and smokier than ever that summer because New York was a two-team town again. In Jersey, everyone either loved or hated the New York Yankees. If you were lukewarm, you got spit out.

A large number of Bayonne people had been born and raised in Brooklyn before the Dodgers moved to LA. They despised the Yankees for winning eight pennants in a row and beating the Dodgers so many times in the World Series. Those recovering Dodger fans always rooted for anybody but the Yankees. So they had quickly latched on to the fledgling Mets—New York's latest franchise—managed by longtime, legendary Yankee manager Casey Stengel. For all Yankee haters, the expansion Mets were it! Even though they stunk.

Hardly anybody in our neighborhood owned a television, so all the men bellied up to the bar at Duffy's to watch the games. Especially on Friday nights and Saturdays. WOR channel 9 televised Mets games. The Yankees were on WPIX channel 11. Between innings, the men would take turns hoisting me up to change the channels back and forth.

Both teams' broadcasts were sponsored by beer companies. *Imagine that.* Met fans drank Rheingold. Yankee fans drank Schaefer. Between innings, a dozen guys often bellowed their beer's commercial jingle.

My beer is Rheingold the dry beer.
Ask for Rheingold whenever you buy beer.
It's not bitter, not sweet.
It's a dry tasting treat.
Won't you try extra dry Rheingold Beer?!

Then the Yankee fans would respond even louder, as passionately as Notre Dame alumni singing the Irish fight song.

Schaefer . . . is the . . . one beer to have
when you're havin'more than one.
Schaefer . . . is the . . . one beer to have
when you're havin' more than one.
The most rewarding flavor in this man's world.
For people that are having fun,
Schaefer . . . is the . . . one beer to have
when you're havin' more than one!

While all this was goin' on, I'm workin' Red Duffy like Sandy Koufax goin' through a left-handed lineup. I must've had ten cokes, five Slim Jims, three bags of potato chips, and a couple of boxes of Cracker Jacks by the seventh-inning stretch. I couldn't finish the game.

Dad must've laid me down in a corner of the room when I passed out in the eighth. By the time the game finally ended, everybody was half in the bag. So they all headed for home—including my father.

I woke up the next morning lying on the green felt of the tavern's well-worn pool table, my head resting on one of those black-and-white-striped pillows without a case. My blanket was a Yankee windbreaker courtesy of Red Duffy, who already had the coffee on, whistling while he cleaned up from the night before.

As I rubbed the sleep out of my eyes, the first thing I saw was my father standing in the tavern doorway, silhouetted against the morning light outside. He took a long pull on a Chesterfield. He hadn't seen me yet; he wasn't there looking for me. He'd only come to Duffy's to pick up a supply of Schaefer for a long-planned all-day outing with some of the guys from the job. Mr. Duffy had already piled a dozen cases in a stack that held the door open. Two of my dad's buddies from Westinghouse, Stanley Proctor and Tom Delaney, began transferring that beer into the trunk of our car parked out at the curb.

"Hey Muzzy!" Red Duffy called from the bar to get Dad's attention and motioned toward me sitting up on the table. I saw surprise register on my father's face before he shrugged and grinned at Mr. Duffy. *No harm, no foul.*

Glancing at his watch, then back at me, he swore under his breath. "Shoot . . . we're late." He paused only a second before deciding. "Com'on, Bobby. You're comin' with us."

I wiped my eyes and rolled off the table. "Thanks, Mr. Duffy."

Stanley Proctor rolled his eyes at my Dad as I clambered into the back seat. "Aww, look who's here."

"Relax, Stan. It'll be good for him seein' the sights of D.C. Besides it's my car."

We drove over to Avenue E and jumped on the turnpike, following the route the three men commuted together for years. We parked on the Westinghouse parking lot in Jersey City. My father called my mother from a phone booth, waking her up to say I was with him. Everybody else at home was still asleep.

Stanley bought me two rolls with butter and a pint of milk before we boarded the bus. After the personal record I'd set for Coca-Cola consumption the night before, it was a good thing for me the chartered coach had a bathroom on it.

We were riding with a busload of my father's black coworkers, fellow union members at the Westinghouse factory, who had invited him to go with them to a giant rally against injustice in the nation's capital. As a Polish-American living much of his life in an Irish parish, Dad had a little experience with discrimination. He knew it wasn't right. He'd seen the way some of his black colleagues were treated at the plant, and he knew that wasn't right either.

I didn't know enough about what was going on in American society at the time to realize how unusual it was that my father and his two buddies (one Polish and one Irish) had agreed to accompany a busload of "freedom riders" to a civil rights protest in Washington. Not until many years later did I appreciate what a remarkable privilege I had that afternoon at the National Mall, perched high on my father's shoulders, looking out over a sea of mostly black faces (almost every man wearing a short-sleeved white dress shirt), and listening to Martin Luther King give his "I Have a Dream" speech from the steps of the Lincoln Memorial. I remember everyone linking arms around us, and the crowd surging like an ocean, as if lifted by his closing words.

> And when we allow freedom to ring, when we let it ring from every village and every hamlet, from every state and every city, we will be able to speed up that day when all of God's children—black men and white men, Jews and Gentiles, Protestants and Catholics—will be able to join hands and sing the words of the old Negro spiritual: "Free at last! Free at last! Thank God Almighty, we are free at last!"

I was so tired and had so much to talk about by the time we got home that night that the subject of where I'd slept the night before never came up.

Three months later, President Kennedy was shot in Dallas. I remember sitting in class when one of the nuns came running into the room crying. The sisters immediately sent all of us home early. In an Irish Catholic parish like St. Vinnie's, everyone took the news hard. We'd proudly considered JFK one of us.

Grandma Walsh had a black and white television set. And since she lived just up the stairs, I spent much of that weekend fascinated by the unprecedented 'round-the-clock news coverage and trying to grasp with a seven-year-old's mind just what had turned our world upside down.

Grandmother was already eighty by that time. No telling how many times over the years I was spared by fleeing up the stairs just enough ahead of my mother's belt or wooden hanger for Nana to slam and bolt the door behind me. She must have known we had more interest in finding refuge or watching our favorite Saturday morning cartoons than in listening to her regale us with stories of her childhood in County Down. But Nana regularly tried to instill in her wee grandchildren a proper appreciation for, and pride in, being Irish. She could never grasp how hard it was for me to be the good Irish Catholic lad she always expected me to be.

JERSEY

For years I dreaded St. Patrick's Day at St. Vincent's School. There would be eight hundred kids in the schoolyard that morning, all wearing something green—a tie, a corsage, a green hair ribbon—as proud evidence of their ancestry. Wanting desperately to fit in, I wore a green clip-on tie my Grandmother Walsh gave me for my eighth birthday. Even so, I took the long way around— past the convent on Forty-seventh Street—trying to time my arrival at school just as the bell rang for lineup.

It seemed like a good strategy at the time. But I got there just a little too early and the Irish Mafia nabbed me. An older kid named Campbell yanked off my tie. No green. My disguise gone, I was now fair game for a beating. O'Connell, Murphy, and Cavanaugh pinned me down and sang, "Hennessey, Tennessey tootled the flute; the music was something grand," banging out the tune on my legs with those hard green plastic shillelaghs (a toy version of an Irish club). Then they dragged me into the darkened church stairwell where they'd already done in my brother and two Italian kids, Mario and Vincent. I took a pounding before the bell finally rang and we all bolted up the steps to the morning lineup.

Campbell had thrown my tie down a sewer drain. So I had to endure the rest of St. Patrick's Day without any green on, subject to the punches and pinches of anyone who noticed. Of course, everyone did.

When I arrived home sore and bedraggled that afternoon, I confessed to my grandmother I had lost my tie down the sewer. But I told her it happened trying to retrieve a baseball.

"If'n it wasn't St. Patrick's Day, I'd give ye a real lickin' myself, I would," she told me as I hung my head and silently suffered her displeasure. I figured the whole painful truth wasn't worth the tellin'. By that time, this halfbreed's biggest worry was how I was gonna eat the corned beef and not the cabbage for supper that night.

I needn't have worried. You could almost get away with murder on March 17.

All the big annual celebrations—Fourth of July, Memorial Day, and Labor Day—provided a great excuse for a party. In the "off-seasons" between holidays, there would be weddings and anniversary parties at the American Legion Hall or the Knights of Columbus. And the bar was always open.

Children didn't worry about the usual limits either. Everybody there was somebody's cousin, so most parents didn't feel the need to pay much attention to us. There would be long buffet tables loaded with homemade desserts to choose from. And no one to force us to eat vegetables. While our parents socialized with friends and relatives, we played games of hide-and-seek under the tablecloths with kids we saw once a year—or didn't even know.

At home we didn't even have tablecloths. We always ate family meals in the kitchen under a permanent cloud of Chesterfield smoke. The "formal" dining room in our house served as my parent's bedroom throughout my entire childhood.

We never had designated drivers in those days, either. Yet somehow our car always "found its way home" from these big celebrations. My mother confesses there were some mornings-after when she'd awaken in a panic and rush to my little sister's crib, clueless as to when or if she'd ever put the baby down for the night.

My baby sister, Mary Ellen, was always there. *But how?* I'm bettin' Nana had a hand in it. *There'n ye go now.*

The Yankees did win the pennant again in 1964. And even more incredible than that, my Uncle Johnnie, Mom's oldest brother, somehow garnered three extra World Series tickets for my father. Uncle John was the only one in our whole clan to graduate from college and break out of the blue collar. He lived in a big house in Scarsdale, was old Joe Kennedy's accountant, and obviously had connections. So my father was able to take my brother Jack and me to see the Mantle-Maris-Howard edition of the Bronx Bombers against St. Louis in Yankee Stadium.

Imagine the thrill. Eight years of age. My first major league game ever. The World Series in Yankee Stadium. Hall of Famer Bob Gibson in a pitcher's duel with New York ace Jim Bouton. The atmosphere was electric. Though the hopes of the Yankee faithful grew dim as we trailed the Cards 1-0 going into the bottom of the ninth.

That's when Dad left Jack and me in the upper deck back of third to go find Uncle Johnnie in the box seats below and have him wave to us. So my father missed sharing the ensuing drama. When Gibson walked Johnny Blanchard and Mickey Mantle came to bat, Cardinal manager Red Schoendienst called in Barney Schultz to relieve his ace. Yankee fans, most of whom were glad to see Gibson go, gave the visiting pitcher a standing ovation out of genuine admiration for his performance.

Mantle promptly homered off the upper-deck arcade in right field. The entire stadium erupted as Mickey hobbled slowly and gloriously around the bases accompanied by a happy mob of teammates and fans who poured onto the field as if the series were already over.

And I was now hooked on baseball for life.

Back in Bayonne that contest was remembered and relived countless times in the months and years that followed, often accompanied by an ongoing debate about why Mantle had staggered so noticeably around the bases after his blast. Of course, everyone knew about his well-publicized knee problems, but legend had it the real reason he had tottered so slowly during his home-run trot was because he'd drunk a pint of Jack Daniels on the bench that chilly autumn afternoon.

If the Mick actually had belted his homer to win the game for the Yankees after downing a pint, that made his feat all the more remarkable in our eyes. And Mantle more heroic than ever.

I learned a lot of hard lessons in the schoolyard. And not just on St. Pattie's Day. I was always tough enough to hold my own in fights against kids my age. But I never stood a chance when a bunch of bullies four or five years older would decide to torment me. Perhaps their cruelest trick was something they called "poling." I never knew for sure if the term originated as a painfully obvious reference to the act itself or if it was a more subtle pun describing special treatment inflicted on Polish boys and other non-Hibernians. Four guys would grab me, then pick me up by the arms and legs, while I futilely kicked and squirmed to escape. The two jokers holding my legs would spread them apart, and then they would all run me right into one of the iron poles that held up the basketball goals.

The pain was so brutal I couldn't walk very well the rest of the day. Which my tormenters also thought hilarious.

Even so, I never ratted on the bullies. That was another important city playground lesson: you never tell. Partly because you knew if you did, chances were good you would get it worse the next time. But mostly you didn't tell because squealing was a mortal sin in our book.

I soon learned that survival in St. Vinnie's schoolyard meant diligently steering clear of trouble and anyone (at least anyone bigger and older) wanting to start it. As well as keeping my nose clean and my eyes wide open at all times. Which meant that I saw a lot that went on. High school guys and some of the local dropouts hung around there, hoping to practice their moves on some of the older girls. I'd often spot them slipping into the darkness of a stairwell on Friday and Saturday nights to make out or steal a drink from a hidden bottle.

Expensive drugs weren't around during my grade school days. But I remember from time to time seeing a few of the older fellas sniffing a carburetor cleaner called Carbona. A guy leaning against the fence or the side of the school building would take a paper bag containing the solvent, hold the open bag over his nose and mouth, and inhale deeply. His head would snap back, his knees would buckle, and more often than not he would begin sagging into a sitting position, temporarily unable even to stand. Chances were when he did get up again and try to walk, he would stagger around so much half the kids on the playground would be staring at him.

In my mind, one word described anyone stupid enough to inhale industrial chemicals for kicks: loser. I didn't need any catchy drug-awareness commercials or a "Just Say No!" campaign to convince me I didn't want to be one of them.

I didn't pick up all the important lessons of life in St. Vinnie's schoolyard. I learned a few things inside the building as well.

My mother always believed in the importance of a good Catholic education. And if she couldn't convince me, the sisters at

St. Vincent's School certainly would. There were two classes in each grade level—kindergarten through eighth—with fifty or more kids to a class. You could hear a pin drop in any room all day long. The nuns maintained complete and utter control through their mastery of two amazingly simple and effective tools: a little handheld clicker sometimes used to bring us to attention, and our absolute fear of ever provoking the wrath of our school's principal, Mother John of the Eucharist. (Eukey was what most of the kids called her, but of course never to her face.)

For reasons I never understood, many of the nuns who taught at St. Vincent's had been given men's names. Sister John Margaret. Sister William Francine. Sister John Thomas. Some of those names did seem fitting for women large enough to play for the Chicago Bears. And I remember a couple of the sisters who must have thought Jesus wanted us all to turn the other cheek just to give them another shot, a better angle to deliver a disciplinary smack.

But it's become far too easy for those of us who grew up in parochial schools to bash the nuns. For every tough sister at my school, there was another sweet enough to have inspired Ingrid Bergman's movie role in *The Bells of St. Mary.* Many of the sisters were genuinely holy women who obviously loved God *and* kids. For me they were constant examples of goodness in a sometimes hard world. They clearly had a connection to something, or someone, I didn't have a clue about.

Sister James Xavier was my favorite. She directed the St. Vincent's Boys Choir. Sixty boys. We were good.

For midnight Mass every Christmas Eve, we'd march into a packed church at St. Vinnie's, proceeding slowly into the darkened sanctuary, each boy clad in a red robe, carrying a single white candle, and singing, "Come, they told me, a rump-a-pum-pum. A newborn king to see, a rump-a-pum-pum ... me and my drum." Mothers and sisters would cry. Even the drunks would get chills and goosebumps as all of St. Vinnie's parish gathered together to celebrate the birth of our Savior. Then my parents, my brothers, Jack and Jimmy, and my little sister, Mary Ellen, would hurry home to open the presents under the tree we'd helped our mother decorate earlier in the evening.

Sister James Xavier also taught me to play the piano. I guess that's when I really got to know and love her. Sometimes, sitting next to me on the piano bench during my evening lessons, she would slip off the stiff, starched-white part of her habit that usually covered her forehead and chin. When I could look up and see her entire face, she seemed so much more beautiful, more human.

I would have gladly done anything Sister James asked. I remember many a summer Saturday morning rolling out of bed and rushing to the church to sing, with just four or five other boys from the choir, the special music for an eight o'clock funeral. There would be a second funeral at nine, and finally another at ten. In gratitude for our devoted service, Sister James would take us over to the convent afterward and reward us with ice cream.

But for her, I'd gladly have sung for nothing.

I think I maintained my crush on Sister James Xavier until I was maybe twelve or thirteen. Then I dumped her for Sally Field, who played Sister Bertrille on *The Flying Nun*.

School came easy to me. The nuns taught us well, and I read voraciously on my own. I forget how many spelling bees I won; the nuns always handed out rosary beads and little plastic saint statues to the winners. Those prizes always seemed to make my mother proud. As did all the E's (for excellent) on my report cards. I was well aware that if I played those cards right, I was "boy uninterrupted."

I got my first paying job at the age of ten. You were supposed to be twelve to run a newspaper route. But when I went to help my older brother one day, I realized nobody was going to check.

So I asked the boss, Mr. Whitey Lapinski, and got a route of my very own delivering the *Bayonne Times* after school every afternoon.

I soon figured out that I would make twice as much money in the same amount of time if I also delivered the competing paper, the *Jersey Journal,* to their subscribers on my *Bayonne Times* route. Neither of my two bosses ever found out.

I'd ride my bike over to Thirty-ninth and Broadway five afternoons a week to pick up sixty copies of the *Times*. Then I'd shoot down to Forty-eighth and Avenue B, where I'd get about the same number of the *Journal*. I'd find a neutral spot to fold my papers, and then I'd run my route from Fortieth to Forty-sixth Streets, providing my customers whichever paper they preferred.

I soon learned to collect from my customers on Friday nights. Everyone got paid the end of every week in those days. If I caught them when they were feeling flush, when they had just begun celebrating the weekend, there was a good chance they'd hand me a crisp one-dollar bill and cheerfully tell me to keep the change.

If I ever waited to collect until Saturday morning, when a lot of people were hungover and grouchy, I usually had to settle for exact change. And since a five-days-a-week subscription to the *Times* was just thirty-five cents, and a week's sub for six days of the *Journal* amounted to fifty cents, the difference in tips from a one-dollar bill made a nice addition to the ten bucks a week the papers paid delivery boys.

The Boulevard, renamed the Kennedy Boulevard after JFK's assassination, was a four-lane residential thoroughfare running the length of Bayonne. While the posted speed limit was twenty-five miles per hour, many people cruised it a lot faster. It was part of a long street connecting Jersey City and Staten Island. So Bayonne was like the nice part of that drive, if you catch my drift.

We had no such thing as synchronized traffic-signals in those days. Everyone got stuck at a red light every ten blocks or so. Even the speeders had to hurry up and wait.

It must have been about 10 P.M. when the bus dropped us off on the west side of the Boulevard along Hudson County Park. A bunch of other newspaper boys and I were returning home from a one-day bus trip to Washington. We'd ridden four hours each way, so we'd actually spent more time on the bus than in D.C. But who knew? And what did we care? We had won our free trip courtesy of the *Jersey Journal* for selling new subscriptions.

"Free" always seemed like a good deal. So we went. Some of the older boys on the block were getting free trips to Vietnam at the time, and they went.

Anyway, two of us got off at Forty-fifth Street where there was no red light, just a bus stop. A classmate of mine, Jackie Racicot, climbed out first. Jackie was a great kid. I thought he resembled Alfalfa from the *Little Rascals* when he stood and sang next to me in St. Vincent's Boys Choir. I usually looked more like Petey, the Rascal's dirty white mutt with the black eye.

I dropped an armful of souvenirs, a tin Spiderman lunch box, and my sweatshirt as I stepped off the bus. So I stooped down by the root of a tree to get organized.

Anxious to get on home, Jackie hurried around the front of the bus to cross the street. He never saw what was coming. Neither did the driver of the car clockin' fifty on the inside lane. I will never forget the sound of the impact. Or what I saw when I raced to where Jackie's body landed almost a block away.

Our boys choir sang at his funeral a few days later. The sisters and the moms all cried. Even Eukey was bawlin'. I didn't know how to cry for somebody else yet, so I just sang as good as I could, in Latin, even though I didn't understand the words. None of us did. We just knew it was sad.

I felt really bad for a long time after that. Kinda guilty. Thinking maybe I shoulda hollered at Jackie to wait when we got off that bus.

Sometime later, I told Sister James about that feeling. One Saturday morning soon after that, she bought me ice cream and we walked over to the Boulevard. We said the whole rosary together, sittin' under the tree by the park, where I'd fumbled my stuff that night. I repeated that ritual many times by myself after that. And I've gone back since without the beads.

TINKER
AND THE FROGMAN

The sun was already down under Newark Bay when I first made contact. Everybody was gone except the two of us.

"Goot. Goot boy!"

Thunk.

"Goot. Real goot. Get square shouldered, face me 'n' catch de ball widjer bat."

Thunk.

"Attsa boy. Three more now. Ready . . ."

Thunk.

"Goot. Bat's high. Lower it. Catch de ball wid it."

Thunk.

"Goot."

Thunk.

"Okay. Ya go home ta eat now."

At nine and ten, I was getting hammered by the older boys on my Little League team. Some of the twelve-year-olds would throw so hard my glove would often go sailing right off my hand with the ball still in it. At the plate, the ball was already in the catcher's mitt before I could swing the bat.

So to keep me from feeling like a total failure, Mr. Ted Hadyka, my first Little League coach, taught me how to bunt. I bunted a lot my first couple of years in organized baseball.

Years later in Chicago, I would teach kids to bunt early. Then whatever is thrown at you, you can return it. A man has to teach a boy that. The coach could be his own father or an old Polish man with a short-brimmed cap.

"Goot boy, Bobbie. Dot one was poifict."

In Bayonne during the '60s, we didn't have to depend on our parents driving us to baseball practice or any other activity. We could jump on our bikes anytime to ride anywhere in town. Yet a lot of days, we didn't even have to leave our block to find enough fun to keep us going till long after dark.

The street in front of our house served as a regular playground. Kids from around our neighborhood gathered there to play "freeze tag" and "scatter" and other games where half the fun was devising elaborate rituals to determine who would be it. "Eenie, meanie, miney, mo" was far too simple for us. Instead, we'd all crowd in close, put one foot in the circle, and then go around the group calling out the cadence and pointing to each person's foot in turn, one syllable at a time:

My mo-ther and your mo-ther
were hang-ing out clothes.
My mo-ther punched your mo-ther
right in the nose.
What co-lor blood did she shed?
Red? R-E-D spells red!

Nice one thet, eh?
And whoever the finger was pointing toward at the end was it.

For ballgames, we usually chose up teams in time-honored fashion. We'd stack hands up the bat. The person ending up with the top hand had to be able to grip enough of the bat to actually twirl it around his head at least once without letting go before he won first pick.

We played a lot of stickball on our street, using an old broom handle as the bat to hit those hard pink rubber balls you could buy at O'Donnell's Sweet Shop for twenty-nine cents. "Twenty-niners" we called them. If you could drive one of those babies past two manhole covers, you were a slugger. But when you broke a window, a dozen pairs of feet would be pounding pavement in every direction, giving a new meaning to the term home run.

Diamond ball was less damaging. With home and first base along the right curb, and second and third along the left, all of the street in front of you was right field. But when you hit between second and third, the houses in left were in play, so you had to "play the wall."

The pitcher underhanded the ball with as much speed and spin as he could muster, trying to land in any part of the diamond-shaped home plate we'd drawn in chalk next to the curb. You swatted at the twenty-niner with your bare hand after the first bounce. And if you missed any pitch that had bounced on the plate, you were automatically out.

What few cars there were in the neighborhood would be gone during the workday. Should an unfamiliar vehicle ever drive up the block and interfere with our game, we'd heap untold abuse on the driver—water balloons, chalked-up twenty-niners, spit, you name it.

But we immediately stopped our game the day a government car turned onto our block and pulled to a halt at the curb in front of the Duffy house right next door. We watched as two uniformed army officers got out and slowly climbed the porch steps. They rang the bell, and when the door opened, they politely took off their hats before going inside to tell Red and Maude Duffy how sorry they were to inform them that their son John had been killed in Vietnam.

We didn't play in the street for several days after that. No one ever told us we couldn't. It just didn't feel like the right thing to do.

Red Duffy never seemed quite the same to me after that. It was like a light had gone out inside him, and he died just a couple of years later.

I felt really sorry for the Duffys when John died; they'd been longtime friends and neighbors. But I never knew what to say to them.

Over the years, it seemed every street in Bayonne had its share of tragedies and heartache that no one ever talked about. Of course, we all knew everyone else's business. Living so close together, especially in the summer with all the windows open, it was hard not to. You could hear what the couple next door argued about, just like you always knew who turned angry and mean when they got drunk.

I remember lying in bed on Saturday nights listening to the ruckus several doors down. The husband would be yelling and swearing. Then you'd hear crashing sounds and the wife would start screaming. Next morning, when we'd attend children's Mass with their kids, I'd try to avoid eye contact for fear of embarrassing my friends by somehow giving away what I knew. Though anyone on our side of the street must have heard it all, no one ever thought to call the police. Playground rules often applied in the neighborhood. "Live and let live" was a policy most people lived by.

Besides, drunken men beating their wives and kids was nothing unusual. My mother's side of the family could have provided any number of poster children for abuse. Her brother, my Uncle Sonny, would burn my cousins' bottoms on the stove and lock them in the closet for hours as punishment. Sonny died following a drunken fall. Then my cousins moved into the projects on Avenue E and would spend a lot of time at our house. Sonny's son Jody was one of the most creative, thoughtful kids I ever knew. Years later Jody put a gun to his own head, ending the emotional torment he lived with.

My mother's sister sometimes arrived at our house late on a Friday night looking like she'd just gone the distance in a heavyweight title fight. Yet every Monday she would return home for a rematch.

My parents never had a physical confrontation. Drinking mellowed my father. Besides, we were all quite certain that if they ever got in a real fight, the Irish woman would win hands down.

Many of the kids in the neighborhood were scared of the Frogman. Their mothers probably warned them to keep away from him because he was a twenty-five- or thirty- or who-knows-how-many-year-old man on the outside (complete with a middle-age paunch and a three-day shadow) yet still very much a little kid on the inside. I knew he was different, and I didn't understand the reason why. That didn't keep us from becoming friends.

We met one of the first times I ever stopped at his house to collect newspaper money. He lived with his parents on West Forty-fourth, one of only a couple of white families on that otherwise black block. He answered the door that day. When I said, "Hi, *Bayonne Times* collecting," he very tentatively stuck out his hand and introduced himself as "Awex."

While his mom went to look for change in her purse, Alex motioned for me to follow him around the side of his house. When he led me through the gate into his back yard, I stopped in amazement.

"Wow, Alex!"

He grinned at my surprise.

"Where did you get all these frogs?" There were hundreds of them all over the small, enclosed back yard.

"Awex catch frogs."

Eventually he told me where he caught them. "Wong docks."

After that, he started walking by our house on his way to the harbor, where big oceangoing freighters docked to unload their cargo containers. Sometimes a few of us would slowly bike along with Alex to scour the shoreline of New York Harbor between the Bayonne long docks and what is now Liberty State Park. Whenever we tired of looking down in the tall grass and the rocky shallows in search of frogs, we had only to stop and lift our eyes to look across a few hundred yards of water to the Statue of Liberty and Ellis Island just to the north.

One summer day, I was playing baseball cards on our steps with Nippy Henderson and Bubblehead Nardone when our game was interrupted by a couple of loud *bangs* and then screams from across the street. When I jumped up, I spotted Alex on the sidewalk across the way. He had obviously been the one screaming, because he was now helplessly flailing his arms, running in place, and shouting "Noooo!" at two older teenagers kneeling on the sidewalk a few feet away from him. I knew the two boys—both lived right on our block and attended technical high school. Bayonne had a lot of these guys—gearheads with long greasy hair, feeble goatees, and fake tattoos.

They were laughing. Alex was crying. And the moment the boys quickly stood up and moved back, I realized what was going on. When they had seen Alex returning from the long docks, they'd stolen the paper bag containing his catch. I could see one of his frogs now—on the sidewalk with a lit firecracker stuffed in its mouth. Alex was absolutely hysterical.

I flew down the front steps and had sprinted halfway across the street before the explosion. *Blam!* Green flew everywhere. One of the bullies didn't even see me coming until I bowled into him from behind. But my righteous fury proved no match for their size and weight. When one of them grabbed me, I bit him. Screaming in rage, he slammed me to the ground and they both put their boots to me.

I don't know if one of my friends called her or if she came out on her own to see about the commotion, but the next thing I knew, my mother waded into the battle. Shouting, grabbing hair, boxing ears, and slapping the backs of their heads, she yanked both bigger boys off me with the ferocity of a mama bear protecting her cub.

Just that fast, the fight was over.

As the sorely chastened boys sprinted up the street, Mom helped me to my feet. She and Alex and I recaptured all the surviving frogs that had escaped from the bag during the fracas. Then she stood with her arms crossed like an angry sentinel, watching until Alex disappeared around the corner heading home. He never came on our block again.

The other boys' mothers didn't speak to my mom for years afterward. But she never caved, because Loretta Muzikowski was a real Lulu.

I was just glad she'd been on my side in that fight.

Summers were my favorite season of the year growing up. Everything was less structured. Since we didn't have school, we could run our paper routes earlier in the afternoon. Newsboys would begin gathering around noon, waiting impatiently for Whitey Lapinski to dole out the bundles of that afternoon's paper. The sooner we got started on our delivery routes, the sooner we got done. (We were practicing the seven habits of highly effective people long before that guy sold a million books about it.)

When the first weighted-down station wagon with its load of freshly printed papers pulled up at Thirty-ninth and Broadway, we'd all pitch in to help.

Joey Burza unloaded. As the one and only "adult" paperboy, Joey got the first few bundles. That was protocol.

Every neighborhood had a special guy like Joey. Professional paperboy was probably the absolute limit of his occupational potential. But he was a pro who ran ten routes of his own. Joey, who was probably in his early to mid thirties, spoke in a high-pitched nasal voice and was the only one of us permitted to call Mr. Lapinski "Whitey."

"Hey Whitey, it's gonna be a hot one t'day. Looks like a real scorcher. Yesireebob! Gonna be a steambath out there t'day."

Joey was only a little taller than most of the other paperboys and had a hunchback. He never used a cart. He delivered the old-fashioned way, full delivery bag over the shoulder. He'd run one route, then come back and load up again, a veritable workhorse for the *Bayonne Times*. He'd been delivering for years when I started and would still be doing it after I grew up and left home.

Amongst ourselves, the rest of the paperboys debated whether Joey was born with a bad back or if he got it from luggin' all those papers. Anyway, if there's a hall of fame for paperboys, Joey Burza is certainly in it.

On this particular day, I helped Joey stack his bundles in the corner of the storefront "office." There was nothing else in there except Whitey's desk and two aging bowling trophies.

Then I crammed sixty papers into the canvas delivery bag bound tightly to the handlebars of my rusty gold Stingray bike, swung my leg over the banana seat, and announced, "I'm outta here, Whitey. See ya, Joey."

"That's Mr. Lapinski to you, kiddo!"

"Okay there, Whi—uh, I mean Mr. Lapinski."

You really had to lean into the pedals with a full load. The good news was the load got lighter with every paper I chucked out. So I finished my deliveries and was flyin' up Broadway toward Forty-sixth before two o'clock.

I stopped by our house just long enough to grab the paper grocery sack I'd stowed in the basement coal bin that morning. My cache contained five mickeys (that's what we called potatoes wrapped in tin foil), matches to start a cooking fire, killies (sardine-sized minnows) in a small glass jar for bait, a collapsible wire-mesh crab cage, and of course, a twenty-niner. It was always good to have one of those. *'Cause hey, you never know.*

I could almost always find something going on between Avenue E and Broadway near the Forty-ninth Street projects. I didn't know what projects were then; I just knew there were usually enough kids around there to get up a good stickball game.

The apartment buildings themselves were three stories high—with flower pots on nearly every window sill. A janitor hosed down the sidewalks and watered the bushes six days a week. The neighborhood was poor, but it was clean.

I found two of the Porche family who were about my age.

We jumped on our bikes and raced back across town, rounding up other members of the Rat Patrol. A couple of kids who went to St. Vinnie's joined us in my neighborhood.

Armed with towels and crab traps, we pedaled in a pack up Broadway to the city line, then five blocks crosstown to Newark Bay. We cut through Marist High School's parking lot and down a bumpy dirt path lined with tall weeds and cattails until we reached our spot.

To us, Newark Bay was the next best thing to the Jersey shore. Our private beach became a mini-Woodstock with kids of all different ages and colors. The black kids in our Rat Patrol attended Washington School on Forty-eighth Street and the Boulevard. But most of the other kids we saw at the beach came from nearby Woodrow Wilson Public School on Fifty-sixth Street. One of them, a black kid I knew as a friend of the Porches, was Randolph "Tinker" Brown.

I joined some guys who were already crabbin'—wadin' in knee deep and flingin' crab traps baited with killies as far out into the bay as they could. We'd cook whatever we caught or brought with us on a campfire I started by adding dry grass and driftwood to the blackened coals left from our previous outing.

I'd just gotten a nice blaze going and was still carefully placing the mickeys in the fire when most of the other boys headed north about a hundred yards to what we called the swimmin' hole, where we would swing from ropes fastened to the concrete girders of the New Jersey Turnpike bridge. Cannonballs, belly whoppers, and jackknives were the dives of choice.

Sometimes the water was deep, sometimes it wasn't, depending on the tides. So the real art was letting go of the rope over the deepest spot near the apex of your swing. If you chickened out or mistimed your release, when the rope swung back, you could slam full force into the concrete girder.

Feeling hungry that day, I decided instead of swimming to concentrate first on cookin' my potatoes and haulin' in crabs. We had heard there was a moratorium or somethin' on crabbing in Newark Bay because of contamination. But we never figured it applied to us. So both the crabs and the smoke from our driftwood stove could have been radioactive for all we knew. Or cared. I'd taken my first bite of a hot mickey, which burned my tongue, when I heard a big commotion at the swimming hole.

Suddenly everybody was runnin' for their bikes like they had broken a window in a stickball game, scurryin' and scatterin' like roaches when the lights come on. Almost before I knew it, most of the Rat Patrol was pedalin' away in their bare feet, sneakers swingin' from the handlebars.

"Boy didn't come up!" someone shouted back in explanation.

I couldn't believe the other kids didn't even stop to pull in their traps. I quickly retrieved mine and tossed it in the weeds by my bike. Then I threw sand on the fire, wasting the other four mickeys, and retreated into the high weeds myself.

Somebody must have run to Marist High School and asked one of the Brothers to call the police, because several cop cars and an ambulance eventually arrived on the scene. When I saw them pull into the Marist parking lot with their lights flashin', I walked my bike the other direction along the shoreline. I didn't want to have to answer any questions—or get in any trouble for being there.

I was still watching from a distance sometime later when the divers pulled the body of a young boy out of Newark Bay. It was Tinker.

"Boy didn't come up."

FIRST HITS

Our summer activities weren't all unsupervised and unstructured. Our city boasted a terrific Little League program. Several days a week, we would grab bats, gloves, and balls and ride our bikes down to the beautifully manicured fields on First Street under the Bayonne Bridge. All that extra practice with Mr. Hadyka paid off. After just a year in the "minors," I made the Army-Navy Surplus Store team in the ten-to-twelve-year-olds league. I played second and outfield the first year. But as an eleven- and twelve-year-old, I caught for that team and forevermore, because I loved being in on every play.

We had twenty-four teams, divided into four brackets, just in that ten-to-twelve age division. The whole thing was a class operation. Sponsors provided nice uniforms and equipment. Your name was announced over loudspeakers when you went up to bat. The *Bayonne Times* even ran box scores and batting averages in the paper every week, which was a big deal to kids when we saw our names in the paper just like our big league heroes.

The summer I was twelve, our Little League regular season ended with our Surplus team in a tie for first place with Bayonne

Plumbing Supply. To decide which team would advance from our division into the four-team tournament to determine the league championship, the officials set up a one-game playoff the following week. Right in the middle of our scheduled family vacation.

My father got only one week of vacation a year. So each summer, our whole family would pack up and go for seven days to the real Jersey shore. We always stayed for the week at my Aunt Tootsie's rental house, a little bungalow in Bricktown, eight or ten miles from the beach. Every morning, we'd climb in the car with our towels, shovels, and beach umbrella to head for the ocean. Dad would let Mom and all four of us kids off at the beach. Then he'd find a place to park nearby and walk over to the Party Time Inn, a tavern actually sitting in the median between the two north-bound and two southbound lanes of Highway 35.

Dad would watch TV, have a few drinks, and hang around the bar at the Party Time until five or six o'clock, when he'd wander back over to the beach. Once he found us, Dad usually took a quick dip himself before loading the family in the car and driving us back to Aunt Tootsie's. That was our vacation.

While it may not sound exotic, the whole family looked forward to our week at the beach. And it meant a lot to Dad that he could provide his family with a real vacation. I knew he had arranged his time off months ahead of time; he couldn't change it. I also knew I couldn't ask the whole family to give up that year's vacation for my baseball game. But my father knew how badly I wanted to make the playoffs.

"Tell you what," Dad said. "We'll all go to the beach like we planned. And on the night of your game, I'll drive you home so you can play."

That's what he did. We drove an hour and a half back to Bayonne—just the two of us. I played in the game that night, we slept at home in our own beds, and then we drove the hour and a half back to the shore the next morning. Which meant Dad was there to watch Paulie Borowicz and me hit back-to-back homers to win the division title 2-1.

I was glad about that. But I was even more grateful years later to realize my father cared enough about my wishes to sacrifice part of two of his hard-earned vacation days to make sure I could play. I have never forgotten that.

Neither can I forget that fall's Boy Scout camping trip, on which I learned that the key to a real adventure was a well-stocked knapsack. Which meant the outcome of the trip was determined at home, where my parents had a liquor cabinet in the living room.

As a child, I was fascinated to learn that when you pulled down the drawbridge-like door, a light went on inside the cabinet, revealing all sorts of bright sparkling glasses right there at eye level. Rock glasses, wine glasses, champagne glasses, and pilsner glasses. These were all for show of course—or in case the priest came over. Everyday kitchen glasses were always good enough for any family and friends who didn't drink right out of the bottle.

Underneath the glass showcase were rows of containers filled with golden liquid of various pales. Of course, we could have pilfered some of the gin or vodka and filled the bottles back to where they were with water. But that might have been too easy for Teddy O'Reilly, the friend who talked me into this caper.

Teddy, who attended public school but lived a short way up my street on the same block as St. Vinnie's, was a huge kid. I mean he was Chubsy-Ubsy from *The Little Rascals* times three. Surprisingly agile for his size, he was a pretty good stickball player. In addition, Teddy was funny and incredibly persuasive whenever he came up with an idea, good or bad.

Every Friday right after school, my mother went grocery shopping. So we determined that that was the perfect time for the two of us to open the drawbridge and execute our plan. Teddy had emptied two clear baby shampoo bottles and cleaned them out pretty good. We filled them up with whiskey by carefully taking just a little from each bottle. I don't know if he was incredibly nervous or just ecstatic in anticipation, but by that point, big Ted was laughin' so hard he was cryin'. When he covered his mouth with his free hand to stifle the sound of his laughter, he snorted snot out of his nose, which he thought even more hilarious.

"Sshhh. We're gonna get caught if you don't shut up," I told him.

The tests we were scheduled to take that weekend—to make Boy Scout Second Class—were pressure enough. We were the two newest guys in the troop, and I was sick of being a tenderfoot. So we hurriedly closed the cabinet and tucked our 80-proof shampoo bottles into the backpacks we were taking to Camp Lewis the next morning.

Mr. Howard Resnick, who owned the local hardware store, ran our troop down at the Jewish Community Center with the help of his older sons, Stewart, Larry, and Mark. Teddy and I were the only two goyim (Yiddish for Gentiles) in Troop 24. But my mother had signed me up for this troop instead of the one that met in the basement of St. Vinnie's because she thought it had better leadership.

My parents considered the Resnicks "real stand-up people." Last time my father had been out on strike, Howie Resnick let my mother charge stuff at his store without a receipt. My mother didn't forget things like that.

The Resnicks caught a ton of flack from people in our neighborhood, more than the Polacks. God forbid there were ever any price increases on shovels or rakes. The Jewish jokes would fly. But the Resnicks were hardworking and fair people. Some ladies even whispered how Mark and Larry could "almost pass for Italians."

Both Teddy and I successfully completed our first two tests after we got to Camp Lewis on Saturday. That night around the campfire, the two of us were in rare form. We started with our best Three Stooges impersonations. I was Moe; Teddy played Curly. *Nyuk, nyuk, nyuk.* Mr. Ed and F Troop renditions followed.

We kept going to our tents to plan our next skit—and to take another swig of shampoo, then chew a stick of gum. We'd never seen Weinstein, Rosner, or the Resnicks laugh so hard. At the end of our performance, we fell backward over our log to a standing ovation.

We wrapped up the evening campfire time with our arms around each other's shoulders, the whole troop. I swear big Ted wuz really cryin' as we belted out the troop song just before taps.

T-R-double O-P Twenty-four's the troop for me.
The pride of all the Bayonne section.
The troop, the troop demands affection.
T-R-double O-P Twenty-four for me.
It's the troop that you like
'cause we always take a hike.
Twenty-four for me!

The next morning was not so great, however. Teddy and I bombed out on both of our tests. Worse yet, we were out of shampoo.

The campfire scene that second night turned from comedy to pathos. All the other Scouts tried to empathize with us, obviously thinking the reason Teddy and I felt so horrible was because we'd failed our qualification tests and were still dumb tenderfeet. Larry Resnick, our official troop leader and an Eagle Scout himself, put his arms around Teddy and me. "Don't worry, guys. Sometimes it takes a while to get these tests right. It's gonna be okay."

Actually, we weren't as dumb as we seemed. I might have still been a tenderfoot, but at twelve years of age, I already knew what a hangover was.

It's okay, Mr. Resnick, I thought. *Next time we'll really "be prepared." We'll just bring more shampoo.*

Teddy and I probably pulled similar stunts two or three times without ever getting caught, which was just one reason it always seemed like so much fun. But we parted ways when we both dropped out of Boy Scouts at the end of that year.

That was about the time my brother Jack and I (sometimes with a couple of friends) started going to Yankee games on our own. We could catch the 99S bus on the Boulevard and take it past Jersey City, through the Lincoln Tunnel, all the way to the Port Authority on Forty-second Street in New York. We'd hop a shuttle train from there to the East Side and transfer to the Lexington Avenue subway line, which took us to a station almost under the outfield. One hour, maybe an hour and ten minutes, from the time we left the house, we could be sitting in our seventy-five-cent bleacher seats cheering for the likes of Mantle, Pepitone, Tresh, and Stottlemyre.

Sometimes we took a little longer than that. Instead of going straight from the subway into the stadium, my buddies and I would make a stop or two at any of the mom and pop groceries there in the Bronx to pick up a few "loosies." Which is what we called beer sold not by the case but "loose," by the individual bottle or can.

Until almost game time, we'd sit on the wooden bleachers of the little park across the street from the stadium, drinking our Schaefer. Two or three beers apiece (at ten cents a can) were usually enough to give a kid a buzz. Then we were really ready to enter the ballpark and commune with the thousands of other Yankee worshipers old enough to afford stadium beer prices.

It actually helped to be a little quiffed if you expected to enjoy a Yankee game in those days. The club went through a number of years in the late '60s and early '70s when even the Mets had better teams. This may help explain why the most fun I ever remember having at a game occurred during a rain delay of a doubleheader.

A thunderstorm hit with little warning. The grounds crew fought a sudden, fierce wind in their desperate attempt to get the field covered. For several minutes, the men seemed to be losing their battle with the tarp. A particularly violent gust of wind jerked the end loose and sent it billowing into the air. One of the groundskeepers trying to weigh down the tarp fell and went slip-sliding across its wet surface.

That looked like so much fun a couple of kids jumped the barriers and sprinted out onto the tarp to try it themselves. *Showtime!* We raced down through the box seats and onto the field. Soon a hundred or more of us kids were climbing and sliding down the undulating tarpaulin like it was some wild ride at a water park. We thought we were in *Schaeffer City.* Even after our added weight helped the grounds crew anchor the covering over the infield, they let us run and belly flop like Pete Rose on a giant slip-n-slide—to the hearty cheers and laughter of the remaining crowd—for several more minutes before rounding us up and ushering us all back into the stands.

By the time I reached the teen years, baseball was no longer my only sport. Sprouting into a 6′ 3″, 125-pound beanpole at thirteen made me such a basketball commodity that for a time I played center on three teams in three different leagues. At St. Vinnie's, I played with my Irish schoolmates. I also played at the PAL (Police Athletic League) with a bunch of black kids. And then, in an attempt to introduce a little height to their league, I was recruited to play on a team at the Jewish Community Center, where I averaged thirty points a game and had a blast.

Our team, Hapoel, won every game by such a big margin that I spent the last quarter or so trying to feed Alan Trachtenberg. The more points Alan scored, the happier Alan's father would be, and the more kosher hot dogs Mr. Howard Trachtenberg would feed me after the game.

My interaction with my teammates at the PAL wasn't always that positive, however.

As a young boy, I knew my father had black friends from work who sometimes visited our home. I had my own black friends I played stickball and rode bikes with. So I'd been oblivious to the racial divisions common throughout America in those days. But there eventually came a time when the civil rights struggle and related events triggered tension and unrest even on our seemingly sheltered little peninsula.

Emotions ran especially high when Martin Luther King was killed. Newark burned. We could see the smoke across the bay. But Dad had been on strike from Westinghouse for two weeks at the time and our family was down to eating canned spaghettios or scrambled eggs for every meal. So our unspoken, uninformed attitude at the time could have been summarized like this: "Sure racism is alive and well. I know there's a reactionary gang in Bayonne called the BONES, which stands for 'beat on niggers every second.' I realize the government has basically said, 'Look, sorry we screwed you for four hundred years; here's a cheap apartment and a coupla hundred bucks a month, okay? We're even now.'

"But ya know what? I'm a kid. My father is outta work and we're behind on all our bills. I've got to walk to school in the snow too. I'm here because my ancestors were getting slaughtered by either Germans or Russians on the one side, or starved by the English and potato famine on the other.

"So go find some WASPs and break their windows, 'cause our gas just got cut off too, and now it's even cold inside."

Nobody wants to talk about this. The history books don't include it. But for years in this country, whenever television news broadcasts showed Alabama's Governor George Wallace and Bull Conner turning the fire hoses and the German shepherds loose on civil rights marchers down south, whenever the newspapers carried pictures of Georgia's Governor George Maddox wielding a pickax handle to prevent "colored folk" from entering his Atlanta restaurant, chances were good that a lot of poor and working-class whites would pay for it in cities up north by getting our heads kicked in.

And years later, when United States senators who could afford to pay thousands of dollars a year tuition to send their kids to private schools voted for busing, it was left to us—the poor and working-class blacks and whites living together in the cities—to iron out the details by fighting it out. So we did. Fortunately, since none of us carried guns around Bayonne in those days, we usually resolved our racial differences with little more than black eyes, stitches, and the occasional broken nose.

I don't remember what created so much tension the winter of my eighth-grade year. I played as one of only two white kids on the PAL traveling all-star team, which competed in basketball tournaments from Philadelphia to Washington, D.C. We all got along and played well enough together on the court, but after practice, it seemed like someone was always trying to get at me by doing nasty stuff like dunking my Converse sneakers in the toilet.

I didn't complain to the coach because of the old playground rule: never tell. *What else is new?* While that didn't make it right, I just figured it par for the course whenever you were in a minority. I thought it was something I just had to put up with if I wanted to play roundball at the PAL.

But I reached my limit the evening one of my teammates took the quarter I always carried for bus fare home. I was tired and didn't relish the thought of walking more than thirty blocks home in bitter January cold. So we got into a fight and most of the team jumped on me.

Someone had a blade of some kind. I ended up in the ER needing more than eighty stitches. I got home so bruised and bloodied that when my father learned what had happened, he announced, "That's it! Forget the PAL! You're never playing on that team again!"

Mom wasn't going to give up that easily. She rode the bus with me to the PAL the next afternoon, marched into the gym, and ripped into our coach for letting me get beaten up by my own teammates. She read him the riot act and made it abundantly clear she would be back if anything like this ever happened again.

You know, it never did. The fact that no one wanted to mess with my mother was one reason. Another reason was that Mr. Farley, the PAL director, introduced me to the club's boxing program that very day after basketball practice.

"Ya wanna fight? Here ya are."

Boxing turned out to be one of the best things that ever happened to me in terms of training, self-discipline, and confidence. You win or lose on your own in the ring.

I would travel with the Bayonne PAL Boxing Team throughout my teen years. And I would train there off and on after that.

Our schoolboy lessons at St. Vincent's were fast coming to an end. Puberty was upon us. But some of us still hadn't mastered the art of not getting caught.

When my best friend, Jimmy Kiniery, flipped up the sides of one of those white sailor hats like Bob Denver wore on *Gilligan's Island,* it looked a lot like a monsignor's cap. Our eighth-grade classroom became his stage. He tipped over Sister Mary Christopher's metal wastepaper basket and climbed up on it, towering over the other forty-some of us now riveted in our seats.

He boomed in a perfect brogue, "All right, boys and girls, I, Father Buckley, would like to give ye m' blessing. So kneel down and empty yer pockets. Bow yer heads and pass the contents t' the front fer Father Buckley, now. In the name o' the Father and o' the Son and o' the Holy Ghost."

Mother John of the Eucharist suddenly appeared at the open doorway behind Jimmy and silently glared at the young "monsignor" still unaware of her presence. We all held our breath. The words "Eukey's coming" could silence the whole school assembly. Her mute presence veritably paralyzed us now.

But Jimmy Kiniery continued in rare form.

"Now girls, if ye darlin's have anythin' ye would like t' discuss privately with Father Buckley, feel free t' come see me personally at the rectory. Or of course, ye may call me directly at et-cum-spirit-two, two, oh..."

That was it for Eukey! She pounced on Kiniery like a Bengal tiger. She had him by over a hundred pounds. Jimmy got jerked off his pedestal by the hair and dragged into the hallway by Atilla the Nun. The entire classroom flinched every time we heard Eukey whale on the young would-be monsignor.

"Wait until your father hears about this!" (That was the kiss of death, as opposed to wait till your mother hears about this.) "You've *(whack)* got *(whack)* detention *(whack)* forever!"

Eukey sounded nearly out of breath by that point. It was hard work chastising squirming thirteen-year-olds while wearing all the layers of a nun's habit.

"Have *(whack)* you *(whack)* had *(whack)* enough, Mr. Kiniery?"

I didn't think that was too tough of a question. I mean, what was he supposed to say? "Uh, no there, uh, Eukey; you might've missed a spot behind my right ear."

But I never heard a response. So it was off to Eukey's office, where the torture would no doubt continue. Poor Jimmy. I shared his pain. Just the week before, I'd been the one out in the hall, caught looking up girls' skirts in the stairwell.

Evidently Eukey didn't follow up on her threat to talk to Mr. Kiniery; we figured that out the next day when Jimmy manned his usual position on the ballfield. You see, if any of our fathers whupped us on Friday night, we were not walking very well on Saturday, let alone starting at second base. All our fathers had forearms like pistons and arms like tree trunks. They could beat the tar out of us, and would, if the sisters ever reported our misbehavior.

Yet there was Kiniery, struttin' and full of chatter as we took the field for warm-ups, joyfully taking all my throws down to second. High. In the dirt. It didn't matter to Jimmy that morning. Like a condemned prisoner who had escaped the gallows, he was one free and happy man.

After we took infield, our head coach, Connie Gallagher, threw batting practice. Mr. Gallagher had starred in both baseball and football at Bayonne High School. But like a lot of men then, he hadn't gone on to play college ball because of World War II.

Anyway, up to the plate stepped Big John Gaddis, our cleanup hitter. At fourteen years of age, John stood well above six feet and weighed over two hundred pounds. He scholarshipped out to St. Peter's Prep and then on to Brown University, where years later I would play football against him in college.

On the first pitch that morning, Big John ripped a searing line drive right off Coach Gallagher's shin. You knew it had to hurt bad, but the coach just hopped on the other leg for a second and kept throwing. He never looked at or rubbed the spot on his shin where Big John's line drive had connected. He never once complained or even mentioned it as he limped through our game that day.

The following Saturday, Coach Gallagher pitched batting practice in a full cast. Turned out the line drive had shattered the shinbone. But he had never rubbed it. And he had never missed a pitch.

IVY LEAGUE BLUES

The perfect antidote for acne was a base hit.

A clutch RBI, a touchdown catch, a nice fifteen-foot jump shot, or a solid one-two combination could cure anything. Or at least ease the pain. Throughout my teen years, sports were a bigger factor in my life than ever.

I probably couldn't have gone to a Catholic high school if it hadn't been for the three-hundred-dollar annual scholarship I received to play basketball. My parents might not have been able to afford all-boys Marist High School with just my Knights of Columbus academic scholarship, which paid the other half of the six-hundred-dollar yearly tuition.

I certainly gave Marist its money's worth on my athletic scholarship. I actually believed I had to earn my keep. From day one, I went for loose balls like a dog after meat. As a sophomore, I served mostly as a tackling dummy in football, but my junior year, I started. When I was named captain of our basketball and football teams and won all-county in football my senior year, it wasn't because I was head and shoulders over the pack. I think I just tried harder than everyone else.

I worked out like a maniac every summer during high school to get ready for football season. I substituted protein shakes for beer through the entire preseason. Once we played our first game, however, Saturday night became the exception to my self-imposed discipline. After every football game, my reward was to "go drinkin'" with my teammates. We didn't say "go party." We called it what it was.

In doing so, we followed the John Wayne–Dean Martin example from so many movies of the day. Fight the battle. Get drunk with comrades. Throw Maureen O'Hara over your shoulder and carry her away even though she "doth protest too much." Wink. Nod.

Everyone seemed to shrug off such behavior with the attitude that "boys will be boys." In the same way, teenage guys who had sex with a girl in the park were "just sowing their wild oats" and were almost proudly considered to be "chips off the old block." Of course, the girls who did it were called sluts. Or worse.

New Jersey had a legal drinking age of twenty-one. But New Yorkers had bought the argument that if eighteen was old enough to die in Vietnam, it was old enough to drink. So our football team's postgame watering hole was Steak and Brew on Twenty-third Street in New York City. The chain later became Beefsteak Charlie's before it went out of business. My buddies and I could have been one of the reasons why.

Steak and Brew was "an all you can drink" restaurant. Every meal included the shrimp and salad bar, plus all the pitchers of beer you wanted, whether you got a very nice steak for $10.99 or the giant cheeseburger for $3.50. Guess which one all ten of us usually ordered?

Our last Saturday night at Steak and Brew, some of the Jersey City guys didn't bring any money. They planned to "dine and dash." Some of us protested, not so much for ethical reasons but because we had been flirting with the waitresses, who pretended to like us. We didn't want to stiff them like that.

But dine and dash is an all or nothing game. If anyone in the group dashes, everyone has to. Since some of the guys had no money, the rest of us had no choice. So after three hours of beer drinking, all systems were go. We pulled out a few bucks to leave on the table for the waitress, ready to slip out the front door and run for the train back to Jersey.

As we waited and watched for a clear path to the restaurant's entrance, a sudden commotion erupted a couple of tables over; a rowdy party of eight guys leaped to their feet and launched their own mad rush for the exit. We were so surprised to see someone else dine and dash that we just sat there frozen to our seats. Before we could think to use the distraction to make our own break, two cops showed up to take the manager's complaint. *What now, Tonto?*

We ordered a few more pitchers of beer to buy time till the crowd began to thin out a little an hour or so later. Then we jumped up, dashed out the door, and sprinted *en masse* for the nearest subway.

Someone must have given a pretty good description and seen where we had headed, because five of our linemen were spotted and apprehended a few minutes later in the Port Authority Train Station. Which could have been really bad if not for the fact that our team captain's father was a Port Authority police captain. The cops let the boys go. But our co-captain still had to answer to his dad.

Not all of the trouble we got into was entirely of our own making.

Racial tensions had not cooled off significantly in the '70s. While riots and fires were no longer raging in front of the cameras, city dwellers knew smoldering feelings could and did flare up regularly.

For Marist football games, our team had to wear helmets on the bus whenever we played the Jersey City public high schools, all of whom were in our conference. After one victory against Snyder High School, their angry fans "rocked" our windows with us on the vehicle. Glass flew everywhere. As we hurriedly pulled out of the parking lot, our coaching staff restrained our players from getting off the bus to retaliate. *Thanks, Coach. We were only outnumbered a hundred to one.*

Ours was the era when many school administrators instituted new scheduling policies. No evening home games for most city high schools. Varsity games began at 3 P.M. But by my junior and senior years in high school, even those precautions didn't matter.

Marist was tied with Lincoln High School for first place in basketball when we played them over in Jersey City. As captain, I led our team into the Lions' Den. (Yes, that is what they really called it.) Four of our twelve players were black. But we were all showered with half-full cups of ice as we made our way from the locker room out onto the floor. During warm-ups, Big John Olsen, Moe Longo, and I gave the finger to the taunting fans. *Great idea, huh? But the three of us played football and were used to the treatment.*

Things only deteriorated from there. With Marist down by ten and with two minutes left in the game, I thought I drew a charge. But the ref ruled blocking on me. When my protest got me a technical foul, a scuffle broke out between our point guard and their star player. Then Lincoln fans stormed the court, giving our team a taste of what it must have been like at the Alamo.

Olsen and I took stitches to the back of our heads. But not before we bloodied our knuckles on the fans. We eventually played out the final two minutes in an empty gym, witnessed only by teammates, coaches, and a sufficient number of the Boys in Blue. When the buzzer sounded, we immediately grabbed our stuff, and the Jersey City police escorted us from the building out to our bus. Showers had to wait till we got home.

Not all my memories from those days involve sports, fightin', drinkin', and chasin' girls. I also studied hard in high school.

Marist wasn't the toughest or most elite school to get into. Still, the Brothers held high expectations in terms of behavior and scholarship; if you repeatedly broke the rules or didn't perform academically, you were gone. Half the guys on my freshman basketball team flunked out by our sophomore year.

Even after I'd discovered girls—maybe *especially* after I'd discovered girls—attending an all-male school like Marist proved to be an advantage. There were certainly fewer distractions during the school day. I enjoyed the sense of camaraderie we all had, in the classroom as well as on the athletic fields. I didn't even mind the dress code, which required us to wear collared shirts and ties to school every day. The rules never specified styles or colors. Some guys would show up wearing a red flannel shirt and a purple tie. That was okay. The administration left that much room for nonconformity.

Not everyone on the school staff was a Marist brother. Two of my favorites were lay teachers who instilled in me a lifelong love of reading and writing.

The paper I remember best was my account of traveling to Washington, D.C., with my father and his friends to hear Martin Luther King's "I Have a Dream" speech. Since I'd been only seven at the time, I had to ask Dad to fill in some of the details. I'd always known my father respected the civil rights leader; I suppose that's one reason I chose to write the paper, which I titled

"The King and I." Still, I was surprised to see Dad get all choked up as he read my final draft.

I hadn't realized until then what an impact my father and his friends must have felt that day on the National Mall when Dr. King spoke of "our white brothers" who, "as evidenced by their presence here today, have come to realize that their destiny is tied up with our destiny. And they have come to realize that their freedom is inextricably bound to our freedom."

It was then that I saw the connection with what had taken place in our home on the evening of April 2, 1968. Just hours after Martin Luther King had been shot down in Memphis, Stanley Proctor, Tom Delaney, and my father solemnly stood in the living room with raised glasses and said, "God save the King." The toasting continued into the night at Duffy's Tavern and long after that.

But many more years would pass before I finally understood how it was that three white, Catholic, working-class guys from Bayonne, New Jersey, seemed to feel a greater loss in the death of a black Protestant minister and civil rights leader from the South than they had ever expressed over the assassination of the first Irish Catholic president of the United States. The amazing, almost mystical personal connection achieved on the National Mall that hot summer afternoon five years earlier was only part of the explanation. The bigger factor was that Dad and his buddies never could relate to the powerful and privileged son of a wealthy, established Massachusetts political dynasty. Not in the same way they identified with a man they saw as an underdog. Like them.

"God save the King."

For a lot of kids, choosing a college is a stressful, difficult, and carefully thought-out decision. Not so for me.

After being named to the all-county football team, I received recruitment letters from a bunch of schools. Not Division I football powerhouses, but fine and respected colleges such as Rice, Villanova, Lehigh, William and Mary, Cornell, and even Harvard. I must have spent a dozen or so weekends my senior year visiting campuses. The athletic departments' recruitment strategies were pretty much the same everywhere. A freshman or sophomore football player would be assigned to escort me around the school and act as my official campus host for the weekend. My host's primary duties seemed to be getting me drunk, introducing me to good-looking coeds, and convincing me good times were to be had if I chose that particular college.

Columbia University made the greatest impression, though. Not only did I get a sampling of the infinite options New York City offered in the way of off-campus attractions, but the morning after my night on the town, I had another eye-opening experience. In the dorm bathroom, standing beneath a stream of water and trying to clear my pounding head, I suddenly realized there was a naked girl under the shower next to mine. At the time, Columbia didn't even have female students. So I have no idea where she came from. But she didn't act surprised or alarmed to see me. I remember thinking right then and there, *I can deal with this.*

I knew almost nothing of Columbia's sterling academic reputation when I applied. Of course, I'd heard of Yale and Harvard. But growing up, I never knew for certain what the Ivy League was, let alone which schools were in it. Even though I had the grades and SAT scores to get accepted.

What mattered most to me at the time was that Columbia University wanted me to play football. The campus was located just across the harbor in the heart of New York City. And the need-based scholarship they offered me would cover 100 percent of my tuition—$4,200 a year. Room and board I could pay for with a part-time work-study job in the campus cafeteria.

I was the first in my family ever to go away to college, so I had no idea what to expect when it came time to report to campus in August of 1974. I packed most of my clothes in a big suitcase, and my dad drove me into Manhattan. Traffic was terrible, as usual. We made a wrong turn. So instead of stopping right in front of the university entrance on Amsterdam, Dad dropped me out on the far side of Morningside Park, and I had to lug my suitcase across what I later learned was supposedly dangerous territory to reach the campus gate.

By the time I enrolled at Columbia, militant student activism and the antiwar movement were well past their prime. Still, there were plenty of people around who remembered the violent student takeover of the administration building back in 1968. The dean who had been shot in the head during that protest still served in the administration.

Half of the students looked like Woody Allen, which probably explains why Columbia didn't do better in intercollegiate athletics, though the football team was mostly made up of characters like me—working class guys who didn't seem to fit the Ivy League stereotypes. Some students labeled us dumb jocks, but the dumbest guys on our football team scored 1200 on their SATs.

I started at tight end for a freshman squad that beat Army and Rutgers. We'd practice hard five days a week and reward ourselves on Saturdays much like we had in high school—by going out and getting drunk. Then I'd force myself to get up every Sunday morning and spend twelve to fourteen hours hiding in the stacks at Butler Library—reading, studying, and making sure I didn't fall behind in any of my classes.

I embraced the academic challenge at Columbia. But the highlights of the undergraduate experience for me were the relationships I developed. I rubbed shoulders with a lot of sharp people. Many of my classmates and teammates hailed from very different ethnic and family backgrounds from mine. Most came from a higher (or much higher) economic strata than I'd ever imagined growing up.

In fact, during a freshman dorm meeting on the fifth floor of John Jay Hall, many of my floor mates included their parents' educational pedigrees when they introduced themselves.

"Hi, I'm Pete from Long Island. My parents both graduated from Yale."

"I'm Arnie, from Boston. My dad went to Harvard, and my mom graduated from Vassar."

When it was my turn, I told the group, "My folks got their education at Bayonne. That's in France. You probably never heard of it."

Columbia exposed me to a whole new world. At the same time, I tried to stay in touch with my roots. I don't think two weeks ever went by that I didn't visit home for a day or an evening, if only to say a quick hi to my parents and my siblings before meeting up with my old buddies to go to a high school ballgame or out to drink somewhere.

I took special pride in my background that year when Muhammad Ali announced that his last tune-up fight before his heavyweight championship rematch with Joe Frazier would be against an old boxing buddy from my hometown PAL—Chuck Wepner, the Bayonne Bomber.

Chuck was practically a neighbor. Not only had I trained alongside him at the Police Athletic League gym, but we played outdoor basketball together in the Bayonne summer leagues during my high school years. Chuck, who was maybe ten years older than I was, hadn't had what you would call a distinguished boxing career—his other nickname was the Bayonne Bleeder. So no one thought he had a chance of winning. Unless you were from Bayonne.

I knew Wepner as a tough club fighter and New Jersey state champion. And I was so thrilled he was getting a shot at the big time that I told anyone who would listen what I believed—that Bayonne's Chuck Wepner could hold his own against anyone. Even Ali.

I remember sitting in my dorm room listening to the fight on the radio with one of my football teammates, Bill Holder, a premed student from Jersey, who was cheering for Ali. When Chuck knocked Ali down in the eighth round, I leaped to my feet and shouted. And for a while after that, I really razzed Holder.

When the fight ended and the judges awarded Ali a unanimous decision, I felt only a little disappointed. Despite all his detractors' predictions, Wepner had finished the fight on his feet. The Bomber had done himself, me, and all of Bayonne proud.

I wasn't the only one who found inspiration in Chuck's performance in the ring that night. A young out-of-work actor happened to see the Ali-Wepner bout. He went home afterward and wrote a screenplay about a ham-and-eggs club fighter from Philadelphia who got his own unlikely shot at boxing glory.

Sylvester Stallone went to Hollywood and made *Rocky*. Chuck received a faceful of new stitches, got his fifteen minutes on Johnny Carson, and a few years later went to prison for a long time.

Another fight took place the spring of my freshman year. The underdog lost that one too. But the stakes were far more personal.

BACKWARD

Growing up, six of us shared the one bathroom in our little house. There was no shower. We all took baths.

For the first eighteen years of my life, that bathroom was always off limits from 6:45 A.M. until 7:15 A.M. every weekday morning. That's when my father got ready for work. He washed up, combed what hair he had, brushed his teeth, and shaved—every day for thirty years. He may have worked in a noisy factory filled with chemical dust, but Dad left for the plant every morning neat as a pin, lunch pail in hand.

In the winter of my freshman year at Columbia, he stopped shaving. By spring he was staying home from work. I knew then he was sick. But neither he nor Mom said anything about it. No one ever mentioned the c-word.

Dad visited the Columbia campus with my mother for my nineteenth birthday in March. We ate lunch together and took pictures in front of Butler Library, leaning on the famous statue *Alma Mater* by William Chester French, who also sculpted the Lincoln Memorial.

After we said our goodbyes, I headed for the stacks to study. At the time, I was so consumed with doing well academically and athletically, so totally self-absorbed, that I hardly stopped to appreciate the visit. Only in retrospect did I realize that was probably the first time in his life that my father ever set foot on a college campus. It was the last time I'd ever see him outside.

In mid-April, my father walked into Beth Israel Hospital in Newark. I was there with my mother to admit him and see him settled into a double room. I even hung out for a while after my mother left.

Big Stanley Proctor came by. He had a pint of Fleischmans hidden in his jacket pocket. Stan poured generous measures into two hospital water glasses, double shots. He gave one glass to my father and the other to me. Then he held out the bottle. We clinked the glasses together.

"Long live the King!"

"Long live the King!"

"Nostrovia, Muzzy. Nostrovia!"

When I went back to see him the following Saturday, I had to carry my father to the bathroom and set him on the toilet. I couldn't believe the change in one week. We still didn't talk about what was happening.

I was just leaving my dorm room in John Jay Hall on May 1, heading out the door to the first of two final exams scheduled that day, when my brother called.

"Mom sez take your tests and come home," Jack told me. "Dad died last night."

I took my tests, then took my bus. I can't say I felt a lot of grief. I was a lot more worried about what would become of the rest of the family. Jack and I were old enough to be on our own, but Jim was only a high school sophomore and Mary Ellen was twelve. Since Dad had been out of work, we were behind on some of our bills. And I remember thinking, *The boat's really leakin'. Now what are we gonna do?*

We buried my father, at age fifty-one, next to his father in Jersey City. Pop had died five years earlier. The Nazis couldn't kill either of them. But cigarettes and factory work did. Smokin' and chokin' right to the end.

Mom immediately took a secretarial job working there in Bayonne for Exxon. She'd been a secretary when she and Dad got married twenty-plus years before, but she'd stayed at home raising kids ever since. I knew she was in essence starting over with an entry-level position, so as soon as I finished my finals, I went home to help out. I worked for the summer on an all-night shift buffing floors and stocking shelves for a big discount store and gave almost all of my earnings to Mom to help catch up the family bills and support my younger siblings.

My second year of college football, I played special teams and second-string end until injuries so decimated our line that I played some as a 200-pound offensive guard on a Columbia team that went 3-6 for the 1975 season. The fact that we didn't field a great football team didn't seem to be a major concern on campus. In fact, most of the student body's attitude toward sports was summed up by a popular cheer that invariably erupted in the student section after we'd fumbled or given up a touchdown. The crowd would chant at the opposition, "That's all right, that's okay, you're gonna work for us someday."

Of course, the athletes cared. And we enjoyed competing against some pretty good football players, such as future Chicago Bear Gary Fencik, who played for Yale, and eventual NFL Hall of Famer Reggie Williams, who anchored the Dartmouth defense. Our own Doug Jackson was named Ivy League Player of the Year that season.

At the end of my sophomore year, I went home and drove a truck for the summer. I knew Mom was really struggling financially by that point and needed help. But she wanted me to go back to Columbia the next fall, so I did.

I called home every night from preseason training to find out how things were going. Just a day before camp ended, after I'd endured the hell of two- and three-a-day workouts in the August heat, my mom told me, "I decided I need a second job. I'm gonna work evenings at Burger King."

"No, you're not," I told her. That was it. I had to go home.

"Don't do it," Coach Billy Campbell advised me. "If you drop out now, you'll never come back."

But I saw no alternative.

Fortunately, when I went into her office to withdraw from school, Dean Roberta Spagnola, who later married Coach Campbell, went out of her way to help. She insisted I fill out all the necessary forms to make certain that "your scholarships will be here for you when you do return."

Back in Bayonne, I partnered with an old Marist teammate and running back, Juan Diaz, to start an independent trucking business. Together we bought a used '69 White full-screw tractor rig that could haul any kind of trailers up and down the East Coast.

I probably learned more about life over that next year than I ever did in school. Bookkeeping, budgeting, planning, and scheduling. Whether we delivered a load to Philadelphia or Miami, we needed to make sure we had another load lined up to bring back from there.

My first use of illegal drugs came driving that truck. Juan and I spelled each other at the wheel. Whenever I got tired, Juan would take over, and I'd try to sleep the best I could, propped up against the door, since our cab didn't have a sleeper.

Because the more time we spent on the road, the more money we could make, we signed on for all the jobs we could. And we started taking speed to keep going.

Black beauties, we called them. You could swallow them, or if you needed an immediate shot of alertness, you would break the capsules open and snort the crystal meth. For me it was never a matter of right or wrong; it was just something we did to keep going.

My family needed the dough.

We'd have made a lot more money if we hadn't rolled the rig and almost killed ourselves one day coming out of the Dundalk Terminal in Baltimore. Juan and I had found the tanker of cooking oil we were supposed to deliver to Newark, carefully checked its number against our manifest, hooked on, attached the lights, and pulled out. But we'd forgotten to lock the trailer down where it fastened to our cab.

When a tanker isn't full, the liquid in it will slosh from one side to the other as you travel, especially on turns. We hadn't driven a half mile inside the terminal when we turned right and several thousand gallons of cooking oil sloshed to the left. Because it wasn't properly locked down, the sudden transfer of weight tipped the tanker, lifting all the wheels on the right side off the ground. Fortunately, just before the tanker-trailer tipped over, the torque snapped off the fifth wheel and our cab righted itself, crashing down with such force that we blew all the tires, broke wheels, and shattered the suspension on the right side of the tractor.

Emergency crews took hours to drain the overturned tanker. We spent more time than that answering questions for the safety investigators and filling out accident reports and insurance forms. After surviving all that, and feeling fortunate not to have our licenses pulled, we still had more than five thousand dollars' worth of repairs to make before we could go out on the road again.

The following summer, Exxon moved the office Mom worked in to western New Jersey and offered special mortgages to any employees willing to relocate. That terrific financial perk, plus the money Mom, my brother Jack, and I had all been able to save, gave her and the family a firmer financial footing. So I could afford to sell my half of the trucking business and go back to school.

The fall of 1977, after a one-year hiatus, I re-enrolled at Columbia to find that the dean was as good as her word. I still had a full-tuition scholarship and a work-study job to cover food, and I had a new place to live—in the huge brownstone Sigma Chi fraternity house a block off campus on 113th Street—for just fifty dollars a month.

I decided not to go out for football again. I was already a year behind my classmates. And I also needed to find the time and the means to make some extra money to help Mom out. She not only had house payments on her place in Morristown, but we had enrolled my sister in a private school there. And my brother Jim was now a freshman at Marist College in Poughkeepsie.

I found a job with real profit potential—right there on campus. Instead of my old position working in the school cafeteria, my work-study assignment that year was assistant manager of the school pub downstairs from the school cafeteria in the basement of John Jay Hall. And later in the year, when the manager graduated, I took over operations and set out to make the King's Pub such an attraction that anyone in search of after-dark action could find it without even leaving campus.

I also formed my own company, named it Action Amusements, and contracted with the manager of the pub (who just happened to be me) to replace the old pinball machines and pool tables with hot, new, faster-paced video games such as Pacman, Space Invaders, and Donkey Kong. Then, as owner of Action Amusements, I'd sit down every week with the aforementioned pub manager to count and divide up all the quarters from the video games. *One for the pub, one for me.* Or sometimes even *one for the pub, two for me.*

Action Amusements proved a very profitable venture for Columbia University. And even more so for me. I learned some important business lessons in the process of running that pub— about giving customers what they want, about managing people, and about the potential rewards in entrepreneurship.

I also learned how to have a *really* good time, a skill I refined with the help of my Sigma Chi brothers and the keg of beer we kept on tap 24-7 in our fraternity house.

My new roommate, Bohdan Sosiak, a large Ukranian from upstate New York, started at offensive tackle for Columbia that year. We called him "Sos," but Bohdan called himself "the Sos." He talked about himself only in the third person. "Man, you wouldn't believe what the Sos did this weekend." Or "I wonder how the Sos is going to play against Princeton this Saturday?"

During our two years together, the Sos made the movie *Animal House* look like an episode of *Captain Kangaroo.* He was elected Quaester (treasurer), and I was elected Annotator. Together we controlled both the purse and the pen at Sigma Chi.

Soon our room contained a color TV, mirrors, strobe lights, keys to a used Gremlin, and the most intricate gerbil habitrail ever seen. And since gerbils are prodigious reproducers, the Sos created a bizarre population-control solution.

A cloud of smoke from Sos's bong usually enveloped our room. Once a month, a crowd of students gathered in the haze to watch Sos (who would dress up in a long white robe befitting the honorable chief judge of gerbil court) as he pronounced judgment in each case.

"Herbie the Gerbil, you have been caught stealing food. I hereby sentence thee to death by the snake." Sos would then place the poor gerbil in a cardboard box with another student's pet boa constrictor.

One gerbil of the month survived a four-story toss into the back-yard snow. *All cartilage.* He became King of the Gerbils, with a little crown and tiny robe courtesy of the Sos.

I declared an end to gerbil court the month a fraternity brother ate one live. Big bets went down on that sentence. But even with my plummeting standards of right and wrong, that was too much for me.

The day before the bus left for football camp our senior year, the Sos announced his retirement from the Columbia team. Pushing 300 pounds by that point, he was not about to go through double sessions in the August heat. Somehow Bohdan made it to his classes and graduated on time. Though I noticed he was completely naked under his graduation robe except for his black socks and shoes.

The Sos had his cake and ate it too. But a lot of guys from our house did not. When we won the campus championship in intramural football my senior year, I was the only guy on the Sigma Chi team still enrolled in school. Several had dropped out to bartend and never returned. One brother eventually ended up in prison for murder, another got shot in a crack house, and one later died of AIDS. Bartender, lawyer, doctor, prisoner, or junkie, my fraternity brothers remain some of my closest friends to this day.

One night after we closed the pub about 3 A.M., some staff and friends gathered in my office for a few beers. One of the students, who I had been told was some sort of Asian prince, said to me, "You look a little tired, a little down tonight, Bob. You ought to try some of this . . ." He pulled out a packet that unfolded neatly like a tiny napkin.

I knew what it was. I'd heard a lot of people talk about coke. I was tired and not averse to trying a little. But when I did, nothing much happened. Not even a buzz. Nothing to get excited about.

Later, when I went back to my room and studied till dawn without getting the least bit tired, I thought, *Wow! That helps.* I usually zonked right out for the night within minutes after closing the pub. And I was always feeling tired. This stuff could be a terrific study aid.

The next day, I went to the bank and emptied my personal account. I took the cash to the prince who'd shared his coke and asked, "Is it cheaper if we buy a lot?"

I only did cocaine that first time.

After that, it did me.

THE BOTTOM

Upon completing my undergraduate program in 1979, I began graduate work, figuring an Ivy League MBA couldn't hurt my resume. Plus I was having too much of a good a time to leave Columbia's campus.

Every night Wednesday through Saturday, I was in charge of fun and entertainment at the King's Pub, which had become a roaring success. To recruit customers, we distributed flyers at the women's colleges in New York. We auditioned and hired popular area bands to provide live music until midnight. Then our DJ, Joe Gerace, a Vietnam vet and grad student, took over and played recorded music until we closed. He shot and played our own videos to music—this in the days before MTV. Each night, six or seven hundred people paid our one-dollar cover charge and packed the place out to drink, dance, and socialize.

In addition to paying me to provide the prime source of campus nightlife, the university also hired me as a resident dorm counselor for an entire floor of undergrad football players. I promptly hired a dozen of them to work for me at the pub. Not only did that make supervision of my charges a lot easier, but it never hurt to have adequate backup—in size and numbers—when any of the customers got a little too rowdy.

The size of my staff kept most would-be troublemakers in line. But it wasn't unusual for a couple of drunks to get in a fight over a girl—or over nothing, for that matter. The trick was to end any violence quickly, before expensive damage could be done to the facilities.

Many a night my Golden Gloves experience came in handy. But the fact is, the biggest, toughest guys anywhere aren't that big or tough after they've had a few. Drunks almost always telegraph their punches. And they usually make enough commotion that they can't surprise you. So when any of our patrons threatened to get belligerent, a quick right to the chin usually ended the fight.

One night a huge football tackle named Jeff started a fight with another customer. He was so wasted and angry, it took me and several of my staff to throw him out. Even then, before he walked away, he turned and punched his fist through the glass window of the door we'd locked behind him.

I made a note to see that he would pay for the damage and thought that was the end of that.

Four o'clock in the morning there was a loud banging on my dorm room door. I opened it and this guy Jeff took a swing at me. I charged him and a real donnybrook began. He was still drunk, but he was big and there wasn't a lot of room to maneuver. I was getting in a lot more punches, but when he grabbed ahold of me, we both went down. Somehow we ended up in the stairwell, tumbling down a flight of concrete stairs. I was dressed in my underwear. He was bigger, stronger, and I realized I was in serious trouble when he got a painful grip on my face. In desperation, I chomped down on the end of one of his fingers. He screamed, let go, and when he saw the bleeding, mangled end of his finger, he swore and went running out into the night.

When I learned he was going to be kicked out of school for attacking a dorm counselor (me), I went to see him. He obviously felt bad about what had happened and about blowing his opportunity at Columbia (the guy came from a working-class family in Charleston, sort of the Bayonne of Boston). The guy was me, really, three years younger. And I felt sorry for him. So I took him to the office of the dean who had been so understanding when my father died. We sat down in her office, my face still puffy and bruised, Jeff's hand all bandaged up, and I told her, "It was a fair fight. I think Jeff deserves another chance. If you let him stay in school, I'll even give him a job working for us in the pub." That's what happened. *Pretty creative sentencing, that one.*

The pub came in handy all kinds of ways.

Where else could I find a job that not only offered me tuition exemption all the way through grad school but provided a steady stream of girls, low-cost entertainment, and no-cost beer four nights a week? On top of all that, I was raking in a small fortune through related entrepreneurial ventures. After installing additional Action Amusements video games in the cafeteria basement, I made money even when the pub itself was closed. Profits from that enabled me to help bankroll another company—Gypsy Sound—in partnership with my regular DJ and good friend Joe Gerace. Since I bought the van, I received a cut of the fees whenever Joe got a gig for a dance or a party. So not only was I going to one of the top grad schools in the country for free and getting paid to throw a huge party four nights a week, but I was also making a thousand dollars and more a week from my related business ventures.

Since I had no expenses of my own to speak of, even after sending a chunk to my mother to help out the family, I had plenty of resources left over to buy a car, take girls out to expensive places, go on Club Med vacations, and do anything else I really wanted.

Every summer throughout college and into grad school, I'd chip in a few hundred bucks along with eight or ten buddies to rent a beach house for the season. We'd work in New York during the week, but on Friday night we'd load up a caravan of cars and head to the Jersey shore. We measured the length of our road trips not in geographical distance but in alcohol consumption. How far is it? About a case and a half.

Once we got to our destination, we spent our weekends playing volleyball or football and drinking all day on the beach, then visiting sports bars during happy hour, and rock-and-roll bars by night. My musical tastes had been developed during vacations as a teenager, when I'd listen to up-and-coming musicians like Bruce Springsteen and the Asbury Jukes playing in Jersey shore bars.

I had discovered rugby my senior year. Then throughout graduate school, I played "A" side flanker with Old Blue, a storied New York club that fielded what was arguably *the* premier rugby team in all of North America. And we were always ready to argue that.

Few things in life seemed more emotionally satisfying than a bruisin' rugby match among friends, after which we'd engage in additional male bonding around a bar, where we'd throw arms over each other's shoulders, lift many mugs of beer, sing spirited renditions of traditional rugby songs, pound each other on the back as we relived new and old athletic accomplishments, laugh uproariously at ribald jokes, and thus ready ourselves for a long night of more drinking and debauchery.

In keeping with the macho image of our sport, we didn't really have girlfriends—we took prisoners. Which was pretty much how I'd operated since high school anyway, whatever it took to reel a girl in. I could write poetry and take long, hand-holding walks with the best of them. So I had a number of long-term relationships, some of which actually overlapped. But even living with a girl wouldn't keep me from going out with the guys on a Thursday or Friday night. I wouldn't show up at home again until late Sunday or maybe even Monday morning, figurin' a dozen roses would make up for anything. If it didn't? There was always plenty of women in New York willing to go out for an hour, a night, or a whole weekend with anyone who was buyin'.

In our minds, we were *carpe diem* guys. Our own men. Rebels who weren't afraid to stretch the limits. We took pride in our ability to stay out celebrating until four in the morning and then suck it up and get to class or work on time. Like we were engaged in some noble quest. Sacrificing ourselves for some greater good.

But that macho, self-sufficient, "I don't care what anyone else thinks because I'm in control of my destiny and no one can stop me" attitude was all an act. Truth was, we were often self-absorbed and out of control. At least I was.

They say one symptom of insanity is repetition of the same action expecting different results. My friends and I should have been cast with Jack Nicholson in *One Flew over the Cuckoo's Nest*.

"Let's meet for a beer after class."

A beer? I've never had *a* beer in my life. I went out for *a* beer and had ten every time.

Then we'd decide to do a *little* coke.

It always ended up the same way. Hiding in some apartment at 7 A.M. Crawling on the floor to watch for movement under the door. Peeking through the curtains. Wide awake and paranoid, waiting for the bogeyman or the cops to show up.

"See that little old lady walking her Chihuahua? I bet she's an undercover narc."

Of course, that's not how we remembered it later.

"What did you do over the weekend?"

"We partied like crazy." We never said, "Actually, we spent five hundred dollars we couldn't afford, just to sit around feeling nervous."

A lot of my friends were somehow able to call it a night at two in the morning. But I'd still be up at 8 A.M. slam dancin' with John Belushi and his crowd at AM-PM, the after-hours club on Murray Street.

I found that once I started constricting blood vessels by snorting cocaine, once I was physically "turned on," it seemed almost impossible to "turn off." Which is why there is no worse feeling than running out of coke at sunrise. Your body might be physically fatigued, but the stimulation will not permit sleep. All you can think about at that point is the next high; anticipation is the only real thrill.

My solution was simple enough. Drink myself into oblivion. Stoli Vodka in OJ was my breakfast drink of choice. *Hey, it's got vitamin C.* But it didn't always work. Fatigued as I might be, I was in my indestructible twenties. So I never seemed to get enough.

The next step closer to the edge was crushing purple microdots (LSD) in the coke and snorting that. Hello Sunday morning. Time to drive to the Jersey shore.

One such Sunday, our caravan melted up the Henry Hudson Parkway and over the George Washington Bridge. There is zero traffic that early on Sunday mornings even in New York. But a cop pulled over the lead car right there on the bridge. The rest of us cruised on by.

The conversation between our lead driver and the state trooper went something like this: "Son, do you know how fast you were going?"

"I'm from New York, your officer."

"I didn't ask where you're from; I asked how fast you were going."

"Uh, sixty-five, sir?"

"Try fifteen."

"Wow! Sure seemed li—"

"Okay, out of the car, boys."

I changed direction during grad school, focusing on government finance. In part this was because one of my profs got me interested in public sector issues, but also it was because I had an internship with the city's office of municipal labor relations one summer. The New York City Fire Department convinced me a graduate degree from Columbia could be just the ticket to a meaningful government career.

I actually got a job and started that career before I received the degree. During my last year of grad school, I held a full-time position in labor relations for the NYCFD, managed the pub, *and* maintained my other business ventures at the same time. I had to give up my pub manager job when I graduated with my master's. But except for that, and a twenty-block move, nothing else really changed.

Without having to study or supervise the operation of the pub, I could make more of an impression on the fire commissioner with my long hours and hard work. And still have more time than ever to devote to my own interests. I continued to play rugby for Old Blue, which led me to one of the people who would alter the direction of my life forever.

I stood on the sidelines with some of my rugby teammates one Saturday afternoon in 1982, waiting for our match and watching Old Blue's "B" side taking on the New York Athletic Club's second team. As play raced down the field right in front of us, an opponent threw a vicious elbow into the jaw of one of our guys, a real cheap shot that connected with such force you could almost hear teeth rattle as the head snapped back. Instead of going down, our guy recovered enough to deliver a roundhouse punch to the thug's head, and a brawl broke out.

When order was finally restored, the referee, who'd seen the second blow but not the one that triggered the incident, added insult to injury by throwing our teammate from the game. That got everyone's attention because ejection from a rugby match is such a rarity. So as our penalized player marched indignantly off the field, obviously furious about the injustice, I turned to one of my colleagues and asked, "Who's the guy got kicked outta the game?"

"That's the priest. Don't know his name."

"No way!" I said. "Not a real priest?"

"That's what I heard."

I had to check this out for myself. So I walked right over to where the guy was still grousin' about the unfair call and offered, "Want a boost?" I held out what I thought was an innocuous ruse—a bright orange child's sippee cup containing an afternoon's supply of cocaine for me and my teammates. The straw sticking out of the hole in the cup gave surreptitious access to the coke right there on the sideline.

He shook his head, "Nah!"

"Someone said you're a priest," I told him.

He looked at me and I saw the corners of his mouth turn up in a wry smile, as if he realized why I might doubt the source of my information.

He stuck out his hand. "B. J. Weber."

"Bob Muzikowski," I said. He had a firm handshake. "Are you really a priest?"

B. J. nodded. "I'm a minister."

A Protestant. Maybe that explains it. I was curious. I'd never spoken to a Protestant minister before.

"You got a church?" I asked.

He nodded. "The Lamb's Church. Down on Times Square."

"No kiddin'?" Prostitutes, runaways, junkies, and tourists were usually the only people on Times Square.

B. J. must have known what I was thinking because he grinned and said, "No kiddin'. Why don't you come and visit us tomorrow? You might find it interesting."

Somehow I suspected he knew I wasn't a regular churchgoer. *Perhaps the sippee cup with the cocaine was his clue.* Except for the occasional Easter or Christmas service with Mom, I hadn't attended Mass in years. I hadn't even seen a Sunday in quite a while.

But I was intrigued enough about any priest who not only played rugby but got kicked out of a match for fighting that when I responded to B. J.'s invitation with a seemingly noncommittal response of "Maybe I will," there was at least a part of me that meant it. And maybe a bigger part of me that wondered just what kind of a racket this guy could be running down on Times Square.

I honestly can't recall if I visited the Lamb's that next day or if it was a week or two later. I do remember B. J. acting pleased, and maybe a little surprised, to see me there. I also remember being surprised myself to discover B. J. had been right; I did find it interesting.

I had attended a couple of Protestant churches over the years when I was trying to impress a girl or make points with her family. But the Lamb's wasn't like any church I'd ever been in. The singing, praying, and preaching seemed even less formal than other Protestant services I'd attended. I wanted to slump in my seat and disappear when people started calling for a fair catch while they sang. But it was neither the hand-waving nor the unchurchlike setting in a beautifully renovated old theater that made this church seem so different.

The most interesting thing about the whole experience was the congregation. Because the regular Times Square clientele—hookers, junkies, street people, runaways—were all there. Sitting alongside business people and spit-shined families that looked like they'd driven in from the suburbs. Then afterward everyone, the homeless and well-dressed alike, sat down together and shared a meal, laughing and talking and even discussing the sermon over a simple chicken dinner. I'd never experienced anything like it.

B. J. invited me to come back. It wasn't long before I did. In part because of what I'd seen there. But also because B. J. was different from any priest I'd ever known. He obviously enjoyed the tough competition and the camaraderie of Old Blue. Everybody seemed to like him. The guys in the club trusted him enough to elect him treasurer. So on the one hand, he fit right in with the rough and rowdy rugby crowd. But at the same time, when he was talking to people, I'd hear him say things like "What do you think God would want you to do about that?" or "What would Jesus do?" and I'd think, *What planet are you from?*

Yet the more time I spent around him, the more I began to think maybe B. J. was real. The guy certainly had an interesting background. Back in the '60s, he'd been active in the SDS underground, which advocated violent acts of protest against United States involvement in the Vietnam War. His closest associates at that time were people whose pictures were regularly displayed in wanted posters on college campuses and in post offices across America.

One day hitchhiking in Dubuque, Iowa, B. J. was picked up by a Trappist monk who asked him questions about his soul and talked about God and Jesus as if he actually knew them personally. When Father William Wilson took his hitchhiker to the New Mellary Abbey to spend the night, B. J. ended up staying and getting to know Christ for himself. "I lived there studying to be a monk for the next six years," he told me.

"No kidding? What happened?"

"The Brothers eventually told me they didn't think I was cut out to be a monk," he said. Then he grinned, "Maybe they knew celibacy would be a problem."

I laughed at that. B. J. continued, "So when I told them I still believed God wanted me to serve him, the Brothers paid my way to attend a nearby Presbyterian seminary. I was ordained and started working at the Lamb's—a Nazarene street mission in Times Square."

I'd never met anyone quite like B. J. Weber. Growing up, I could relate to a couple of devout young priests who served at St. Vinnie's for a year or two before moving on to other parishes. But the senior priests were all older men, proper and dignified, who lived alone in a huge rectory, drove Cadillacs, drank hard, and even played golf on their days off.

B. J. and the other ministers at the Lamb's seemed like regular guys. They actually lived upstairs in the run-down old building that housed their church, enjoying the same humble living conditions they offered to the people they took in off the streets. That too impressed me.

But not enough that I thought I needed to make any serious changes in my life.

Until Christmas of that year—1982.

I'd finally gotten the Christmas spirit. Nine o'clock in the evening, December 24. I loaded all my presents for the family in the trunk and hopped in the car to drive to Jersey. I planned to attend midnight Mass with my mother and then go back to the house to open presents with her and my siblings.

On my way out of town, I happened to drive by Guys and Dolls, a topless bar on Forty-sixth and Lexington. I glanced at my watch. *Hey, I've got time to kill.* So I stopped for a nightcap. Or two.

Evidently Christmas Eve isn't a busy night for topless joints. A couple of Russian sailors and I were the only customers in the place. So it didn't take long to get served. Or to strike up an acquaintance with one of the dancers on break who brought me the drinks. We ended up in the VIP room and then later at her place.

Next thing I knew, a late morning sun was shining. By the time I got into my car and raced to New Jersey, my family had phoned every hospital they could think of and had the police on the lookout for my car.

Even in my hungover condition, I realized this marked a new low for me. I'd just blown off our entire family Christmas tradition. Sure, I felt incredibly guilty. But why make everyone else feel bad on Christmas? So I made up a story I figured my mother would like to believe.

"I was up studying when I fell asleep right in my Lazyboy chair. The next thing I know it's 10 A.M. Christmas morning. Hey, sorry. No big deal. Oh, here are your presents and . . . the drinks are on me."

I had some good Catholic guilt working by that point. And I knew I was guilty as charged. With a trunkload of unopened presents on Christmas afternoon, it was impossible not to see my hedonistic attitude for what it truly was: pure, unadulterated selfishness.

That reality check, continued tension with my live-in girlfriend, and being forced to contrast my self-centered lifestyle with the compassion shown to others by the people I met at the Lamb's Church made me determined to change what had become an ingrained pattern of behavior.

I couldn't count the number of times, over the next few months, that I went to work hungover on Monday morning and vowed to myself "Never again!" I'd go for two weeks, working out like a maniac, and not touch a drop. At my office, I'd be churning out the work.

Then I'd go out for "a drink" on Thursday night, drink enough to depress my system, do "a little" coke to bring me up, counter that high with more booze, and wake up again on Sunday or Monday wondering what I'd done and who I'd been with.

I knew exactly what Mark Twain meant when he wrote that he never understood why people thought it so hard to quit smoking. He'd quit at least five hundred times. I have no idea how many times I quit "partyin' so hard."

I meant it every time.

For a while I thought maybe I could balance the scales of justice and somehow compensate for what I was coming to see as my inadequacy, failure, and selfishness by doing something for others. So I volunteered to work with kids at the Lamb's. One night a week, I'd go down to their building on Times Square to play ping pong, go roller-blading, or play chess with some of the kids there. Maybe on Saturday pick up a couple of them at a welfare hotel and take them to a park or a ballgame. Trying to introduce at least a small measure of normality into the lives of kids who had drawn the short stick in life, many of whom didn't have homes or even families, some of whom had been physically, emotionally, and sexually abused for years already.

While I greatly admired the care and compassion I saw in the people working at the Lamb's, I always felt I fell short of their model. And I never really understood their motivation. If anything, my volunteer ministry at the Lamb's, while in some ways satisfying, made the rest of my life seem more painful and hollow than ever.

Like the Friday night I walked eight-year-old Jeremiah back to the seedy SRO (single room occupancy) hotel where he was living with his mother and two sisters. Mom was heading out the door juzst as we drove up.

"You leavin', Mama?" Jake asked, disappointed. "Where ya goin'?"

The answer was obvious in her short dress, high heels, and makeup. But the poor little kid didn't have a clue. His mother first glanced at me and then told him, "Mama's gotta go to work, baby. You go on up to the room and go to bed." And she walked off down the street, probably heading over near the Lincoln Tunnel, hoping to hook up with some guy like me from Jersey coming into the big city with big plans to get drunk, do drugs, and find someone to have sex with.

The irony hit me as I watched her walk away. Here it was nine o'clock on a Friday night. I'd spent the last couple of hours trying to bring a little enjoyment into the life of this poor kid. But if the rest of the night went as usual, I'd go to a bar, get drunk, do some coke, and if things got really twisted, five or six hours later I could be the one hookin' up with Jeremiah's mother and not even know it.

I'd like to say that thought sent me home sober. But it didn't.

It wasn't easy going out for a good time after doing volunteer work with kids whose lives were in sad shape because of what addiction was doing to their families. But somehow I managed. Mostly by not thinking about it.

Something I didn't understand kept drawing me back to the Lamb's. B. J. knew I was struggling. He told me God could give me the strength I needed to change. I wanted to believe him. And more than once when I'd decided to quit but was too trashed to find my way home, I called B. J. and he got out of bed to come drag me out of whatever rat hole or sewer I'd fallen into, drive me back to my place, and let me sleep it off.

During this time, I let B. J. talk me into joining a small, weekly early morning Bible study with a handful of guys—a former South American drug dealer, a former heroin addict and male prostitute, an architect, and even a couple of professional football players with the New York Jets. It seemed the least I could do after B. J. had been so friendly to me. Plus I enjoyed having coffee and hanging with such an interesting assortment of "religious" characters. Even though I still conveniently called myself an agnostic. (Agnostic sounded less certain than atheist, and I hadn't taken the time to be certain about anything.)

All my life, I'd spent as little time as possible seriously thinking about such subjects as God and faith and guilt and forgiveness. I'd always thought doing so might spoil my fun by making me feel bad.

The truth is, by this point in my pilgrimage, a lot of other things were making me feel bad. My longtime girlfriend finally decided she couldn't take any more emotional imprisonment and made her escape. Wild weekends that started on Thursday and too often continued into Monday began to take their toll on my labor relations job. I thought I could see the handwriting on the wall, so I resigned my position with the New York City Fire Department before the ax fell.

I didn't have another job lined up. At the age of twenty-eight, my whole life seemed to have reached a new low that winter when B. J. made me an offer I couldn't refuse. He invited me to go with him and some of his friends down to Washington, D.C., in February to attend the National Prayer Breakfast. The president, most of Congress, and a lot of other bigwigs would be there.

Since I knew he knew I didn't have anything better planned, all I could say to B. J.'s invitation was, "Sure, why not?"

A bunch of us took the train to Washington the day before the breakfast with plans to stay with a friend of B. J.'s. But that night, I opted to have dinner in the suburbs with an old girlfriend and her husband. When they went home to bed after one bottle of wine, I was just warmin' up.

I'd never been to that town in my life and didn't know a soul there. But it didn't take long to find the local nightspot. And it took less time than that to get a stool at the bar and have a lot more than "a drink."

I have no idea how long I'd been there when the fight erupted. I didn't know who started it or what it was about. But I'd had enough to drink by that point that when one of the club's big bouncers waded in and started pounding on a smaller customer, I joined the fray. It wasn't my fight, but I jumped in anyway. My first punch got the big guy's attention. When he turned and started for me, I attempted a Clint Eastwood move, swinging from a chandelier to knock down my opponent. But the chandelier pulled out of the ceiling and came crashing down on our heads. As we scrambled to our feet, another bouncer grabbed a beer bottle by the neck, broke it off on the edge of the bar, and came right at my face. When I instinctively reached up to ward off the blow, a shard of glass went all the way through my left hand. Almost simultaneously, I grasped a heavy glass beer mug in my right hand and swung it with all my might into the side of yet another bouncer's head.

With the remains of a Heineken bottle still imbedded in my hand, I bled profusely. But I was in a lot better shape than the other guy when the paramedics took him to the hospital. The police escorted me. And as soon as a jail doctor stitched me up, the cops threw me into the local lockup for the night.

I never made the National Prayer Breakfast. Instead I was charged the next morning with battery (for fighting), malicious destruction of property (for yanking down the chandelier), and assault with intent to maim (for smashing the bouncer's face with a beer mug). The no-nonsense judge set bail at $100,000 and sent me back to the can.

It took B. J. and his friends a couple of days to finally find me and arrange the ten grand the bondsman needed to guarantee my bail. I still remember the sense of relief I felt when I handed the prison jumpsuit to the guard in exchange for my own clothes. As I walked out of my cell, B. J. looked at my heavily bandaged hand

and then at the rips in the knees and elbows of my Brooks Brothers suit. He didn't say a word.

But when one of his buddies, Brad Curl, exclaimed, "Praise the Lord!" and gave me a bear hug, I thought, *Who are these guys?*

TURNAROUND

Of course, I wasn't home long before I decided to have a drink. And then do a little coke. Which made me so antsy I had to drink more to come down. I must have fallen or tripped or something and landed on my hand, because I'd ripped open my wound again. I tried to staunch the bleeding myself for a while, but about the time I decided I needed medical attention, the phone rang.

I never picked up when I was high. But for some reason I did this time. And it was my conscience calling.

"How ya doing today, Muz?" B. J. wanted to know. After a two-day high, I wasn't even sure what today was. But I told him where I was going.

The emergency room at St. Luke's Hospital on 113th Street seemed awfully busy. I took a seat and filled out a yellow form attached to a clipboard. One of the questions asked, "Are you currently using any drugs or medication?" I wrote, "No." *Absolutely not. Not any more. I flushed it all down the toilet three hours ago.*

The bleeding in my left hand had stopped by the time B. J. strolled in. He glanced at my hand and then looked into my eyes. He knew what had happened. So I was expecting him to say something like, "Hey, don't blow my bail money!"

Instead, he sat down beside me. For the longest time, he didn't say anything. Which was hard for B. J., who ordinarily could talk the bark off a tree.

After what seemed like an eternity, he looked over at me and asked, "Can I pray for you?"

"Yeah. No question." I figured, *It can't hurt!* What else could I say? The guy had shown up in the ER on 113th Street *and* was still holding the bag for my bail-bond money. I wouldn't have bet on myself at that point, so B. J. clearly had more faith in me than I did.

"Repeat after me," he said. "Lord, thanks for sending your son, Jesus, to die for my sins that I might have life.

"I repent of my sins.

"And ask you into my heart."

I'm pretty sure I said something colorful about my sins during my part. But B. J. never flinched.

Lightning didn't flash as we prayed. I heard no voices when we finished. But it was suddenly as if I had new eyes looking around at my fellow patients in that waiting room. The kids I saw in that ER were obviously really sick; it wasn't their fault they were there. But most of the men in that room were like me; my problems were self-induced.

I knew seeing a doctor wasn't going to help me. So I handed the clipboard back to the receptionist. Together B. J. and I walked out into the daylight.

I bought him an early lunch at Tom's (*yeah, the place from* Seinfeld) on 112th Street and Broadway. I wolfed down a club sandwich as if I hadn't eaten in two days. I commented to B. J. that I'd lived in that part of New York for almost ten years but had never eaten at Tom's in the daytime. I'd always been there at four or five in the morning, coming down off a bender.

B. J. invited me to church, saying, "We're open twenty-four hours a day, too."

I laughed. But I was already doing some serious thinking as I said goodbye to B. J. at the subway and started walking back to my apartment. Asking for forgiveness seemed easy enough, especially when I was undeniably guilty. It was the "go and sin no more" part of Jesus' message that posed the problem.

I spent the next two hours furiously cleaning the apartment, wondering if this time could be different. Hoping and praying that somehow this time *would be* different.

The phone rang. As soon as I recognized Dave's voice, I figured, *Well, here's my first test!* Dave V., a wrestler from New Jersey, had been a big drinkin' buddy of mine who dropped out of college so many times it took him eight years to graduate from Columbia. I hadn't seen him in over a year. But I could tell something was up; Dave sounded different.

After a little small talk, I asked why he was calling.

"I don't know," Dave told me. "I just hadn't seen ya in a while and wondered if we could get together."

I figured it would discourage him, but I told him I'd decided to make some changes in my life. His reaction surprised me.

"Then why don't we get together tonight?" Dave told me he had quit drinking and drugging altogether and was meeting a bunch of guys who had done likewise at 6 P.M.

"Uh ... okay," I agreed, and he gave me the address. Even at the time, I thought his phone call seemed like an incredible coincidence.

"You sure you don't know a guy named B. J.?" I asked.

A little while later I caught a cab across town.

As we shook hands, I noticed Dave was sporting a healthy tan instead of his old yeller. Together we descended a damp stairwell into the basement of a church, then sauntered through a nicotine haze to the front row. *Nowhere to hide.*

The density of the cigarette smoke reminded me of dinnertime around our kitchen table growing up. *Stuck with the Camels here, though.*

I glanced at my watch, wanting out before this thing even got started.

A ruddy-complexioned businessman in his thirties sat at a little desk directly in front of Dave and me. He wore his white dress shirt sleeves rolled up, his tie loosened, and the map of Ireland on his face. He looked good and tired, like he'd earned his fatigue. The guy coughed, and all conversations in the room, which had quickly filled up behind us, ceased immediately. *They all must have had nuns in grade school.*

"Hi. I'm Jack and I'm an alcoholic."

"Hi, Jack," the whole group responded in unison.

Great. Nice fraternity this.

Jack said, "Let's have a moment of silence for all those still sufferin' out there."

Never mind "out there." I'm sufferin' from smoke inhalation right in here, Jacko.

"Is there anybody here for the first time?"

I raised my hand. "Here."

Everybody clapped.

Jack stared at me like I was an idiot. "So-o ... ah ... what's ... uh ... your name?"

I stared back.

"Do you have a name?" he asked.

"Bob."

Everybody said, "Hi, Bob," and clapped for me again.

Great! Double applause for the guy up forty-eight straight hours.

"But I'm not like you guys. I've just got a few problems to fix. I got in this bar fight, so ... uhh ... well ... actually I've gotten in about thirty bar fights, so ... umm ... uh, I'm just here to celebrate my thirtieth bar fight."

Some guys in back laughed. Dave mumbled something about me being a wise guy, but everybody said in unison, "Keep coming back."

Again Jack smiled at me, like I was a very welcome idiot.

A woman to my left started to read out loud, "Our story discloses in the usual way: What we used to be like; what happened; and how it is now.

"Remember that we are dealing with alcohol—cunning, baffling, and powerful. Without help, it is too much for us. But there is one who has all power—that one is God. May you find him now.

"Half measures availed us nothing. We stood at the turning point. We asked his protection and care with complete abandon. Here are the steps we took, which are suggested as a program of recovery."

Then the woman began reading the Twelve Steps. I read silently along with her off the banner hanging on the wall behind Jack. "1. We admitted that we were powerless over alcohol, that our lives had become unmanageable."

Dave leaned over and whispered, "Muz, remember the night we were stopped at a red light outside the Lincoln Tunnel and two of the girls working the corner of Forty-fifth and Tenth called to you by your first name? I'd call that unmanageable."

Had my life really been that unmanageable? Let's see, drunk or hung over since Boy Scouts, lost my job, broke, down to 165 pounds, up on serious charges in criminal court, facing jail time. And all this despite an Ivy League education, a wealth of opportunities, and a measure of past success.

The reader had moved on to the next step. "2. We came to believe that a power greater than ourselves could restore us to sanity."

That presupposes I had some sanity to begin with! I was always so rational. Such a clever rogue with a drink in my hand, a straw up my nose, and my arm around a girl who was never anybody's sister or daughter.

The reading continued. But I couldn't get past the third step right above Jack's head. It said, "3. We made a decision to turn our will and our lives over to the care of God as we understood him."

That's what I did this morning with B. J. in the hospital on 113th Street. But did that count? I was really still out of it from the night before. *Who is God as I understand him?*

Then Jack began to talk. He had the floor, no interruptions. He started to tell my story. As I listened, I was getting really ticked off at Dave for telling this stranger the details of my life. Then it hit me, *Jack doesn't know me from Adam. Jack is talking about Jack. It's just my story too. That's all.*

Jack finished speaking and everybody clapped. A few other people raised their hands and talked about what Jack had said and how it related to their day.

Then, guess what? Everybody clapped.

We all held hands in a circle.

"Whose Father?" Jack asked.

"Our Father, who art in heaven, hallowed be thy name. . ." we all responded.

A lot of people started hugging each other. A few slipped out of the room and headed back "out there." I sank back down in my front row spot to reread the Twelve Steps banner. I didn't feel like leaving.

I dunno, maybe the smoke reminded me of my father. I stayed down.

I was home.

I did keep coming back.

For the next ninety days in a row, I attended one of the five thousand AA meetings held every day in New York City. *Must be a few problem drinkers out there.*

I filled my drinking time with a lot of other things—working with the kids from the welfare hotels through the Lamb's Church, training for distance running with handicapped athletes from the Achilles Track Club, real conversations, and a *lot* of meetings. At church as well as AA.

The combination helped me to work through and make sense of the rest of those steps—all the way up to number twelve: "Having had a spiritual awakening as the result of these steps, we try to carry this message to alcoholics and to practice these principles in all our affairs." There was no way I could ever have done that—and I'm not sure I could have even understood the spiritual dimension of the program or the direct references to God in five of the steps—without the reinforcement I got from my new faith.

A lot of my old buddies gave me grief about not going out drinking with them. Some of them told me they wanted me to be "Muz again, not born again."

They just couldn't seem to understand all that was happening to me. But then, neither could I.

When my case finally went to court, I pled *nolo contendere* on all charges. What else could I say? I knew I was guilty.

The judge sentenced me to a short stay in the county jail and ordered me to recompense the bouncer I'd clobbered with the beer mug. The Old Blue newsletter carried a short item saying, "Muz will miss some of the upcoming matches due to his temporary relocation in the Washington, D.C., area."

I guess some people reading that just assumed I had a new job. And after I got out of jail, I did.

For over a year, Tom Mitchell, a Northwestern Mutual sales director, had been trying to talk me into starting my own insurance business. Tom laughingly told me later that he knew I was a born salesman because every time I blew off an appointment with him, I'd had him absolutely convinced I was interested enough to show up the next time.

Now I figured my legal problems had put an end to any chance of working with Tom. But I went to him and confessed what I'd done, how I'd decided to turn my life around and had gotten sober. To my surprise, Tom not only believed in me enough to give me a start in the business, he told me his story and agreed to be my AA sponsor—the guy I called when I just needed to talk, when I was struggling and wanted a little encouragement from someone who'd been there.

I couldn't believe my good fortune.

The insurance business made perfect sense to me. The way I looked at it, only three things can happen to anyone. You can die too soon, live too long, or become disabled. At Northwestern Mutual, the highest-rated company in the industry, we provided protection for all three. My job was just to spend time with people, find out their needs, and see how I could help them.

I liked my new work and soon became convinced I could be good at it. I made some of my initial sales to friends. Rugby buddies who were finally settling down and starting families. People I'd gone to school with at Columbia whose careers had already begun to take off. A good percentage of my clients worked on Wall Street; they were growing families with growing insurance needs, and they were successful enough to afford sizable policies.

Once I got my business started, it required only long hours of hard work and persistent networking to multiply my clientele. Some banks, brokerage houses, and union welfare funds soon became large accounts for me.

So it didn't take long for business to take off. And I was pleasantly surprised to discover how much less income it took a single

guy to get by on—even at New York City prices—if he wasn't
blowing a couple of grand a week on booze, drugs, and women.

At that point, it would have been easy just to refocus my energies and resources away from the selfish pursuit of pleasure into
business success and making lots of money. But people at the
Lamb's Church continued to challenge me in terms of my lifestyle
and my values.

Father William Wilson, the Trappist monk who had so influ-
enced B. J.'s life, visited the Lamb's to speak about his new ministry in South America. A few years earlier, he'd received
permission from his abbot to leave the Iowa monastery on a personal pilgrimage to Bolivia. He wanted to know Christ better by
obediently following Jesus' example of residing among and loving
some of the world's poorest people. He moved into a small hut
among the Quechua Indians in the mountains of Bolivia, spend-
ing his days mostly in prayer. But before long, the local people
began bringing their sick to Father William's door. Despite having
no medical training, he compassionately offered what comfort and
care he could. The needs seemed so great that through his contacts
in the States, he raised the resources to start and staff a small
clinic. It wasn't long before someone asked him to take over an
orphanage in a nearby town, and his mission grew to include a
school and a second orphanage. When I met him, he'd come to the
States to visit friends and raise additional support to help even
more people.

After I heard Father William speak, a few of us went out to
eat with him and spent the evening talking. I was so impressed by
this man's sincerity, his gentle humility, love for God, and obvious compassion for people that I wanted to spend more time with
him. So instead of my usual winter vacation at some tropical

island paradise, I flew to Bolivia and lived for two weeks in a hut with a dirt floor and helped put a roof on a mission building, rebuild a wall for a school, and light a village playground. I also spent time just talking with and working with and worshiping alongside Father William's Quechuan neighbors. I was so moved by the incredible needs I saw in Bolivia, so inspired by the work of Father William and his Amistad Mission, that I made several trips back to Bolivia over the next couple of years.

Knowing my past penchant for cocaine and that country's reputation for cultivating coca plants, I'm sure some of my old friends suspected I had my own smuggling operation going. *Muz and missionaries? Who are you kidding?* But the only high I found in the Bolivian Andes was a true spiritual mountaintop experience gained from being with the holiest man I'd ever met. Father William had obviously found joy, fulfillment, and peace living among some of the poorest people on earth and demonstrating God's love simply by sharing life with them and being the kind of caring neighbor who did anything he could to meet whatever needs he saw around him.

In Bolivia I saw the challenges Father William and his helpers faced just to get from village to village. So back in New York, I used a commission check to make a down payment on a brand-new, four-wheel-drive Ford Ranger and had it shipped to the seaport nearest the mission—Arica, Chile. Then I flew down to drive it across the border to Bolivia. Only to have the customs officials tell me they didn't have the "proper paperwork" to release my truck. After three frustrating days staring at my truck parked right there on the dock (I had scheduled only ten days for the whole trip), it finally dawned on me that "proper paperwork" was a euphemism for a bribe. And that the customs agents weren't going to approve the truck's release until I forked over a sizable amount of money.

The only money I had with me had been donated to the mission. That was Father William's money. And I had already paid for that truck. Paperwork or no paperwork, that truck was mine. And soon to be Father William's.

Suddenly indignant over such blatant extortion by the customs agents, I sidled over to the impounded vehicle, waited until I thought no one was watching, jumped in the cab, started the truck with the extra key I'd had in my pocket all along, drove right off the dock, and headed straight for the mountains.

The customs agents must have remembered where I said I was going. Because when I reached the Bolivian border a few hours later, the Chilean military border guards had a description of the vehicle and of the tall, skinny gringo who had "stolen" it. An armed guard ordered me out of the truck and escorted me to a locked interrogation room, where I sat alone for the rest of the day trying not to think about the horror stories I'd heard of Americans forgotten in wretched South American jails. I could imagine my old friends, convinced their suspicions had been confirmed: *Muz and missionaries? Yeah right.*

Finally one of the guards returned, handed me my keys, and said something in such rapid Spanish that I couldn't understand. I didn't ask him to repeat himself. Nor did I bother pulling out my Spanish-English dictionary. I just rushed across the border into Bolivia as fast as I could. I never did find out why the Chilean government let me go.

I was soon reminded how important that truck would be for the mission. Within hours after I reached Father William in the village of Aramasi, a Quechuan man walked into the clinic carrying a critically ill baby. That wasn't unusual; two out every three Quechuan babies die before the age of two. The only hope for little Herman's survival was to get him to the nearest hospital as quickly as possible. So we jumped in the truck and I drove this worried father and his desperately ill baby to the town of Cochabamba, a rugged three-hour drive out of the mountains.

When we finally raced into the ER, baby in arms, hospital officials took one look and refused admittance. They wouldn't even examine the boy because he was Quechuan. "Go down the street," they instructed us. "To Dr. Abdon's house. He sometimes treats Indians."

I was furious, but there was no point in arguing. We needed to get help. When we arrived at the doctor's house, I took Herman from his father's arms and headed for the door. I wasn't going to take no for an answer this time. Fortunately I didn't have to. The woman who answered the door invited us in and told us the doctor would be right with us. The grim-faced physician took one look at that baby and immediately began injecting fluids. But it was too late.

Herman took his last breath and died right there in my arms. The father wept. The doctor had done all he could.

I drove back up into the mountains with that Quechuan father sitting beside me, cradling his dead child in his lap. A little while after we got back to Aramasi, I walked to the family's hut to pay my respects. There I watched as the grief-stricken mother gently bathed her baby's body one last time in a pail of brown river water and then laid him carefully in the lettuce box that would serve for a casket.

Like a lot of my peers, for most of my life I had dismissed "religious people." *They're all hypocrites!* That certainly was not true of the soft-spoken, gray-bearded priest I watched living among the poor in Bolivia. What I saw in Father William was an amazing demonstration of AA's twelfth step. His spiritual awakening had led him to carry his message of new life to others, and he powerfully communicated that message by simply and practically living out his faith "in all of his affairs" in front of his neighbors.

I came home from Bolivia having been forced to rethink my image of "religious hypocrites." What religious people had I been looking at? Mother Teresa? Martin Luther King? What about B. J. and the Lamb's Church staff, who not only cared for runaway child prostitutes but also ministered to the very first wave of those men and women who contracted and died from AIDS?

All along, there had been Christians right around me in New York who practiced their principles in all their affairs. Just as there were people with staggering needs right outside my apartment door.

When I accepted an invitation from the Webers in the fall of 1985, I didn't know B. J. and his wife had invited twelve single guys and twelve single women. I arrived at the party with Tom O'Connor, a blind friend I trained and ran with for the Achilles Track Club. Tom, who had lost his sight as a teenager, was from Bensonhurst in Brooklyn, so he still had a lot of "the Fonz" in him.

The two of us had this rap we did. I'd wear dark sunglasses and hold his fold-up walking stick. With Tom on my arm, I'd "accidentally" poke a girl with the stick and he would ask the girl, "Ever been on a blind date?"

We tried our shtick on an attractive twenty-something girl with a southern accent. She laughed at our line and we all started talking. Turned out she was a banker from J. P. Morgan trading the British pound and spent ten hours a day at the trading desk. The girl was beautiful, confident, and successful. *Perfect for Tommy and me, right?*

As usual, Tommy snuggled up to her pretty good. He had perfected that *Scent of a Woman* blind guy rap long before Al Pacino won an Academy Award for it. "Man, Bob, dis Tina Wells broad like got the whole stinkin' Bible memorized," Tommy whispered when she got up to get a soda. "I really like the accent, though, dontchoo Bob? What's she look like?"

"Oh, she's really got a nice personality, Tommy. Too bad about those giant warts and all that weight," I told him with feigned sadness.

I'm 98 percent sure Tommy knew I was puttin' him on. Because when Tina returned, Tommy challenged her to come out and run with the Achilles Track Club, then left us in search of greener pastures.

For the next two hours, we were alone in the crowd.

"How'd you meet B. J.'s wife?" I asked.

"At a Christian Women's Fellowship meeting. How did you meet B. J.?"

"He bailed me out of jail so I could serve as entertainment at his parties." She laughed.

We had polar opposite backgrounds, one Tennessee "y'all" and one New Jersey "you guys." But she didn't seem to care. We laughed out loud together, shared a disdain for pretense, and had a similarly intense faith in the teachings of Jesus Christ.

At the end of the evening, Tommy and I dropped Tina off at her apartment, a walk-up on Fifty-second and Ninth. It seemed like a pretty seedy neighborhood for somebody making a six-figure income.

"It's all I need, really, just for sleeping," was her explanation.

Then we dropped off another passenger. After leaving Tina to me, Tommy had spent the last two hours of the party enthralled with this very nice lady who had a voice like Marilyn Monroe. I just didn't have the heart to tell him she was probably older than his mom.

I couldn't get Tina out of my mind those next few days. I knew even then this was one girl I would never be able to take prisoner.

But I also realized I didn't really want to. I was looking for a different kind of relationship now.

Two weeks passed before Tina and I could get together for our first "date." You'd have thought I'd never gone out with a woman before. I wasn't sure where we should go or what we should do.

So I had this brilliant idea to cook out and go to the Columbia-Dartmouth football game with some of my college friends. This promised to be an interesting cross-cultural experience for a University of Tennessee graduate who was used to watching her alma mater play Alabama in front of 100,000 fans.

Tina was ready when I picked her up. My compadres were not. When I knocked on their door on 108th Street, everybody was still up from the night before.

While I was bummed out about having cooked a lot of chicken that nobody could eat, I wasn't surprised. In the past when I'd planned to attend a Columbia game with this bunch, we seldom made it any farther than the tailgate party.

Anyway, this time six of the revelers piled in the car with "my date," smokin' pot and tryin' to mix peppermint schnapps in her hot chocolate. I figured this would be our first and last date since these were some of my best friends. And *my* newfound sobriety was not *their* problem.

But Tina was a very good sport about everything. And after the game, she took some pretty good shots in a rugby–touch football game with the boys. She could catch and run and didn't throw like a girl.

The following week, she arrived in Central Park as a volunteer runner with the then-fledgling Achilles Track Club. Conversation can get pretty deep when you are dropping off people your own age who are blind and confined to wheelchairs for life with muscular dystrophy but are still training to run marathons. You go right to the heart.

Anyway, Tina and I went deep quickly.

A few months later, we stood on the Verrazano Bridge at dawn for the start of the New York City Marathon. Tommy and I ran together and finished under four hours. Tina ran with Yvette, her new African-American girlfriend with cerebral palsy. They were out there for over six hours but finished the marathon. We all cried.

When Tina and I ran together, I had trouble keeping up. She was way ahead of me in other areas, too. She'd been a committed Christian since she was a young teenager growing up in Brentwood, Tennessee. I was still trying to figure out what spiritual commitment means. So when we started going to church together at the Lamb's, I really appreciated her perspective on what I was hearing and learning there. I'd never read the Bible or even prayed with a girl before, so I was surprised by the difference that made in our relationship.

The night we'd met at B. J.'s, I told her enough of my story that I figured I'd scare her off. But she wasn't nearly as concerned about where I'd been as about where I was going. Somehow she was able to overlook all the garbage from my past and simply accept me for who I was now. That was almost too good to be true.

In the fall of 1986, Tina won a Rotary Scholarship, took a one-year leave of absence from Morgan, and moved to Scotland to pursue graduate studies in international finance. We dated long distance, and on Christmas night in Stratford-upon-Avon, England, sitting on the swing at Anne Hathaway's cottage, I asked her to marry me. I even had it snow in the background. Believe it or not, we also made the commitment not to have sex until after we were married. Which, by the way, wasn't easy but did prove incredibly romantic.

That following May, we ran the London Marathon together. Tina's goal was four hours, so of course we finished in 3:59 and change. Tina's parents and my mother flew over to meet and to watch the race. Alas, my mother had a few ales during the race and afterward informed my fatigued fiancee, "You'll be divorced in two years, sweetheart." Which in Gaelic means "welcome to the family."

In October of 1987, my rugby club, Old Blue, scheduled a game in Nashville. We played the Tennessee All Stars at noon. My best man broke his ribs and I received a concussion and a black eye, but I married Tina Wells that night anyway. B. J. presided.

Tina and I rented an apartment in Battery Park City. It wasn't nearly the rent-control bargain I'd had on the Upper West Side. But there were just too many memories associated with my old place. I didn't think it was right to ask Tina to reside with my ghosts. Just living with me would be tough enough.

And it would have been, if it had been just me.

The Lamb's homeless shelter always had an overflow. So starting the day we returned from our honeymoon, it seemed as if one or another of the guys I sponsored was crashing on our living room sofa. Tina was great about it. But I began to think there was just too much history for us to stay in New York.

So when my sponsor, Tom Mitchell, moved to Illinois to start a new Northwestern agency, I began to think about relocating. When in the spring of 1988 Tina found a job in foreign currency trading with the Chicago branch of Union Bank of Switzerland, we decided we would make a brand new start together. So we headed for the peace and quiet of the Midwest.

IN THE BIG INNING

I don't know how many times I passed that empty lot at the corner of Sedgwick and Division without giving it a thought. I certainly never could have imagined how it would change our lives.

Tina and I lived just a few streets away on the 1400 block of N. North Park in one of those large two-story frame houses wedged tight in a row—like so many of the residences built in the old working-class neighborhoods of America's cities in the first half of the twentieth century. Even with three bedrooms, two baths, and a nice big fireplace, this duplex was so much less per month than we'd been paying for our Battery Park City apartment in Manhattan that it was the first and only place we'd even looked at before we signed the lease and moved to Chicago.

We called the area SoNo (for south of North Avenue), and living there was considered "pioneering" at the time. Our block was long on kids, vacant lots, and different-colored people. We knew when we moved in, back in May of 1988, that we were every bit as close to the infamous Cabrini-Green housing projects to our south and west as we were to Chicago's prestigious Gold Coast to the east. But having spent my entire life in the New York City area, and having lived for years at or around Columbia in Harlem,

I was used to such demographic disparity. I knew that in a city, three blocks could be a world away.

A key factor for us was convenience. On that score, we had an almost perfect location. We lived within a block of Joe Guinan, who had been a college roommate and was one of maybe five or six people I knew in Chicago before we moved. LaSalle Street Church, a socially active evangelical congregation we joined, was just a few blocks over. And the Mustard Seed, the neighborhood AA chapter where I attended the 6 A.M. meeting at least once a week, occupied an old firehouse on Wells just four blocks away. It was a very short jog to the city's beautiful lakeshore parks and just over a mile and half from the downtown offices where Tina and I worked.

The only real drawback to the place was the elevated train track just a few feet across the alley from our garage at the back of the house. We'd first seen and agreed to rent the place on a Saturday afternoon, a time when mass transit runs a limited schedule. It wasn't until we'd moved in that we realized the north-south Ravenswood line averaged a train every ten minutes Monday through Friday. The rolling thunder of the Chicago Transit Authority would shake and rattle every inch of our house from attic to basement. The greatest, and perhaps only, plus side of that was that our oldest children, who would be born while we lived on North Park, could, and still do, sleep through anything.

Several mornings a week, I'd leave home about dawn and run down to the Loop to work. I could only go south on my street for a short way before confronting the old shoe factory lofts and a sprawling Oscar-Mayer meat-processing plant, which forced me to jog west for a block. That little detour took me past stables housing the horses that pulled the fancy carriages full of shoppers, diners, and tourists who took in the sights and enjoyed the nightlife along North Michigan Avenue's Magnificent Mile every afternoon and evening. I never could get over the irony of living in the heart of the inner city at the end of the twentieth century and yet, lying in bed on warm summer evenings with the windows open, being able to hear in the quiet between passing El trains the clip-clop of horses' hooves and the soft whinnying just a block away.

At Sedgwick I turned south again and ran for two blocks past the west end of the meat factory, the muscles in my legs slowly loosening as I began to breathe through my mouth in a deep, steady runner's rhythm. Just south of the meat plant, I came to an abandoned patch of urban landscape encompassed by an eight-foot chain-link fence.

That vacant lot covered a city block. And like most such deserted property, it had attracted the usual urban detritus—faded and flattened trash bags with loose edges flapping in the breeze, broken bricks, bottles, cans, disposable diapers, and an occasional piece of broken furniture so forlorn no self-respecting street rat would seek shelter under it. All that distinguished this empty lot from any other in the city were the two backstops at opposite corners of what was evidently once a ballfield. If you looked carefully at the tufts of crabgrass, dandelions, and clover growing through the trash, you could detect the outline of an infield. A fine plastic mesh covered much of the area, someone's long forgotten and futile attempt to keep the field's loose sand and dirt from disappearing up and down the nearby streets of the Windy City.

I occasionally wondered who had ever played on that field. But I have to admit that as I ran to work most mornings, I paid a lot less attention to that junk-strewn lot than I did to the cluster of buildings looming to the south and west of the basketball courts on the other side of Sedgwick. Many of the windows in the checkerboard concrete highrises had been boarded up, giving some Cabrini-Green buildings the battered countenance of a broken-down old boxer who'd lost too many teeth in too many fights.

Yet thousands of people still lived in the government housing project, the vast majority of them children under the age of eighteen.

Rumor had it that the police often refused to answer calls at Cabrini-Green, long considered one of the poorest and most violent of Chicago's urban neighborhoods. The newspapers regularly carried reports of nearby shootings. And there were times on summer evenings with our windows open that we heard gunshots beyond the neighing and whinnying in the nearby stables.

Some of my coworkers and neighbors thought it insane when they learned my route to work took me through Seward Park, just south of Carson Field, on the east edge of the projects. But I can't say I ever felt threatened.

The reason there are no bad neighborhoods at 6:30 A.M. is that most of the people who make them dangerous are, like Dracula, afraid of the light. By the time the sun begins to rise out of Lake Michigan every morning, they have fled, retreating into the shadows and the darkness to wait out the dawning day.

Not that I, or the residents of Cabrini-Green, ever witnessed the rising of the sun as I ran to work. Those Gold Coast highrises to the east, with their front-row, luxury-box apartments, robbed our view of Lake Michigan and claimed dibs on the sunshine, casting long shadows over the less expensive neighborhoods to the west until the sun finally cleared their rooftop swimming pools and satellite dishes much later in the morning.

The streets between our home and the nearby projects seemed much brighter—definitely more alive—in the afternoons. Anytime we had halfway decent weather, the action on the basketball courts across from Carson Field overflowed onto the sidewalks. Kids not old enough or good enough to be shooting hoops would skateboard, roller-skate, jump rope, or play hopscotch up and down the sidewalks in the afternoon shadows of the Cabrini-Green highrises.

On many a warm spring or summer evening, I might see a handful of kids from the projects playing tag or just racing each other on the abandoned field. A few times when I noticed a handful of youngsters playing a pickup game out there, I joined them. More often, I'd go out and play stickball with the kids right on our street. And whenever I did, I remembered playing in city streets and parks when I was a kid and thought, *The kids in this neighborhood could use a real Little League to play in.*

But for more than two years, I never really considered doing anything about it. I was busy with my company. A majority of my clients remained in New York, so I was commuting back every couple of weeks. On top of all that, we'd had a baby girl in 1989, and Tina had left her day job to become a full-time mom. So it wasn't as if we didn't have anything else to do.

Then early one evening in August of 1990, I took my infant daughter, Sammie, for a walk after supper. I pointed out the horses through the fence at the stables, and when we turned south on Sedgwick, I noticed a group of kids who seemed to be engaged in a scrimmage game of baseball down on the abandoned field. So I kept walking that direction.

Drawing closer, I realized the pitcher was an African-American man, the first adult I'd ever seen out here playing with the kids. With Sammie in my arms, I slipped through a gate opening and stood at the edge of the littter-strewn field observing the play.

When batting practice ended a few minutes later, I walked out to the pitcher, who looked a few years my senior, and stuck out my hand. "Bob Muzikowski."

"Al Carter."

We talked only for a couple of minutes. I explained that I lived just the other side of the Oscar-Mayer factory and commented that I hadn't ever seen any other adults on this field before. He told me he had organized a tournament for some of the neighborhood kids that year and hoped to be out there on a regular basis.

I asked if he could use some help. Al acknowledged the obvious; he had a shortage of volunteers. So I went back the next evening, and the next, to umpire and even play some ball with Al and the kids.

Al and I discovered we were both avid runners. So we met a week later and ran together. Several times during the fall, we met in a parking lot over at the lake and put in a few miles up and down the lakeshore. At 5'10", 150 pounds, Al was a phenomenal competitive miler who ran faster than me, despite being fourteen years older.

I learned Al had grown up in the Cabrini-Green neighborhood, had been in the military for a while, worked for the city's human services department, and in his spare time ran the Al Carter Youth Foundation—organizing sports tournaments, working with and trying to help kids any way he could on a shoestring budget. He said finding help was always a challenge. Neighborhood men, who could be relentless critics of any newly organized venture, rarely volunteered to do anything.

I suggested teaming up. With my baseball experience and business contacts downtown and his history in the neighborhood, maybe we could do something together. Al was skeptical. When I pressed him, he told me that over the years he'd encountered more than his share of liberal white do-gooders who talked about wanting to do something for the poor black kids in the projects. Most of them never got beyond the talking stage. He said even those who did never lasted long.

In effect, he said, people used the kids. When they didn't find enough of the warm, fuzzy emotional rewards they'd dreamed of, they cut out. Which meant their plans and programs too often ended with disappointment and disillusionment for everyone.

Still, I kept talking about improving "Carson Field" and maybe organizing an official Little League program for the kids of

Cabrini-Green and anyone else who wanted to play. I felt confident I could personally contribute and raise enough money to do the thing right. "We'll have team uniforms and everything."

That fall and winter, whenever I ran past that eyesore of a city block, I saw beyond the weeds and litter. I envisioned a real baseball league. Real diamonds in the rough. Not a whimsical ballfield planted among cornfields in the Iowa heartland but a true oasis of green grass carved from the heart of Chicago's concrete jungle.

I couldn't get that picture out of my mind. I was convinced that if we built it, kids would come.

Al agreed to give the league a try. I visited Little League Baseball headquarters in Williamsport, Pennsylvania, and applied for a charter. We were officially approved and incorporated as the Near North Little League. And as a means of promoting black heritage, Al insisted that all the teams in the Near North Little League would be named for African tribes.

Al was league president, I served as VP, and Tina, who was expecting our second child in June, was co-treasurer. A friend of Al's served as our first commissioner, and two friends of mine, a banker and a real estate broker, made up the rest of our executive committee.

Carson Field actually belonged to the city and had once been the site of a high school. Before the school was torn down, it had served as the setting for one of Hollywood's first attempts at portraying "modern" urban youth culture in the 1975 movie *Cooley High*. And since the Chicago Parks District at the time did little to maintain ballfields in poor neighborhoods, there was no one to stop us from sprucing the place up and using it for our new baseball league.

Tina and I showed up with a bunch of our friends to help clear off the fields on a couple of Saturday mornings early that spring of 1991. A few of our volunteers were professional colleagues and business contacts from downtown. Some I knew from the Mustard Seed. A few were fellow members of LaSalle Street Church.

Cleaning up an entire city block that's been neglected for years seemed a formidable job. But I believed the neighborhood kids deserved to have just as nice a field to play on as suburban kids did. And all that would be required was a little hard work. *No big deal!*

Frankly, I was happy to be anywhere. It's just that since I got sober, I'd been sitting up front and actually paying attention to a lot of sermons and AA meetings. And believed what I was hearing.

AA taught me I could live a sober life one day at a time; so I figured anyone could clean up an abandoned field one broken bottle or one crushed can at a time. And help one kid at a time. My faith and the examples I'd witnessed had taught me that being a Christian means truly believing what Jesus said about loving my neighbor, the Golden Rule, and honoring him by serving all my neighbors (not just the ones who could serve me back). This meant reaching out to those around me who needed help and encouragement with some form of practical ministry.

I was definitely not a preacher or a social reformer. But the teachings of both my Christian faith and AA convinced me that God calls us all to be better neighbors by practicing our beliefs "in all our affairs." To go out the front door and actually "do" the Bible was just life.

While I had no illusions that I would change the world, I had no doubt that God wanted me to play baseball with the kids of Cabrini-Green. They were, after all, my neighbors. Carson Field was the nearest "park" to my house. Plus I'd had many great coaches from Little League through college. So how could I not "coach back?"

The Chicago Parks District was so impressed with our cleanup efforts that they provided city dump trucks to carry away the piles of refuse we'd collected. Then they hauled in several truckloads of dirt to cover and soften our hard and unforgiving infields.

The diamonds began to take shape. All we needed were the kids to play on them.

I wanted to have flyers announcing sign-ups distributed in every parochial and public school classroom in our area. The Catholic school posed no problem, but I needed to find a way to go into the public schools with a positive introduction.

That's when I walked into the office of inimitable state representative Jesse White. A longtime community activist himself, White, who has since become Illinois' secretary of state, had a special passion for kids' sports programs. For forty years, he's made a name for himself coaching and training the Jesse White Tumblers, a troupe of youngsters whose high-octane acrobatics have wowed pro athletes and fans alike at sporting events and special performances throughout Chicagoland and around the country.

Jesse said he'd personally take care of the flyer problem. He made the call that enabled volunteers to place flyers in every nearby school.

I still vividly recall the sense of uncertain anticipation I felt the morning of our first official sign-up day. As I gathered up our card table and scrounged around in the garage for a lawn chair for Tina to sit in as she handed out registration forms—she was great with child—I hoped we'd have as many as fifty youngsters turn out. Enough to field maybe four teams.

When we set up the registration table on Carson Field at 9 A.M. that early April Saturday, Tina and I were the only people there. By ten I began to wonder, *If we get enough kids for only one team, who will we play?*

But by eleven, we'd had an encouraging trickle of interest. A handful of kids stuck around to play catch with a bunch of used gloves and balls I'd brought for the occasion. When I began hitting infield grounders, we gradually gathered a small crowd. And by afternoon, the registration line stretched down the Sedgwick Street sidewalk.

Even working together, Tina and I and the friends who came to help us couldn't keep up.

Some of the younger kids came with their mothers or grandmothers. But most of them picked up the registration forms and raced home to get a parent's or guardian's signature. "When our season startin'?" some kids wanted to know.

By the time we folded up our card table and loaded it in our station wagon that afternoon, we had more than two hundred children signed up to play in the Near North Little League—plus another fifty or so kids who'd played with Al the year before. On the one hand, I was thrilled. On the other, I had this panicky realization like the captain in *Jaws* had when he first saw the shark: *I think we're gonna need a bigger boat!*

DIAMONDS
IN THE ROUGH

Tina and I spent the remainder of the weekend trying to imagine what it would take to organize, finance, equip, and run a league of twenty to thirty teams. The first and biggest problem was obvious. We needed more volunteers.

By Monday morning, I'd come up with what I prayed would be an effective recruitment plan. I had my secretary call around to florists and collect forty boxes for long-stemmed roses. But instead of flowers, we put a Little League bat in each box.

Before the day ended, we had them delivered to every stockbroker or futures trader I'd had as a client—mostly at the Mercantile Exchange. We sent them to several law firms I'd done business with and to a few top executives I'd met in brokerage firms and commodities trading companies. The attached note read: "You are invited to a get-together and buffet at the River Club at 200 South Wacker Drive this Friday at five o'clock. You must bring your bat. If you are unable to come, please send someone else with your bat."

I signed it "Batman," figuring a creative approach would arouse curiosity and get me a good crowd at the club on Friday. I was right. More than thirty guys showed up wondering who Batman was and what this was all about.

Most of them were surprised when I stepped to the front of the room. I reported the overwhelming response to sign-up day. I asked them to remember the opportunities they'd had growing up to play baseball and all that experience had meant to them as kids.

I told them we needed individual or corporate sponsors for each of maybe twenty teams. And that we'd estimated a $675 donation would cover a team's bats, balls, gloves, and catcher's equipment, along with matching hats and uniforms. A quick show of hands indicated my sales pitch had hit home. Almost twenty guys committed to sponsor a team.

Then came the true test. "But we need more than money to equip these teams," I told them. "If you agree to sponsor a team, we also need you to coach it."

Most of the people there signed on that day. Many of those coaches and even some who didn't coach went out and recruited friends, colleagues, and an occasional subordinate to help. We soon had enough coaches to divide up names and assign rosters for twenty teams. And as we'd expected, once we started practicing regularly on Carson Field, a lot more kids showed up and were added to our teams.

I sponsored two teams and coached the one in the nine-to-twelve-year-olds division. Both of my teams were named the Northwestern Mutual Life Pygmy; nobody else wanted to take that tribal name.

I met Brian Dixon the very first day of practice. He was eleven years old that year. Like half the members of my team, he expected to be the star.

Those initial practices were pretty wild. It takes more experience than most of our volunteer coaches had to organize an efficient and productive baseball workout for a bunch of kids. We all learned as we went along.

The vast majority of my boys had no experience with organized ball. So even those with the most athletic ability had a lot to learn about baseball fundamentals.

Fortunately, we had a lot of qualified volunteers. My assistant coaches were Dr. Bill Vranos, who'd played baseball at Boston College; Dave Lilja, who played tight end for Indiana; and the only father who helped out that season, Willie Naugles Sr. Together we kept the kids so busy during practices that we saw tremendous improvement in a very short time.

I had administrative snafus to iron out in addition to my coaching duties. Creating regular practice and game schedules for the whole league was a bear. Tina's considerable math and organizational talents proved an immense help. So was a Merrill Lynch trader by the name of Bill Harrington, who played a huge role in creating the league schedule.

With twenty teams divided into two age groups, we figured we would have to schedule at least two games a night on each of our two diamonds during the week and a full slate of games all day on Saturdays. Even then there was no way to get a complete season in without playing under the lights.

Fortunately the field already had them. But keeping those lights turned on proved to be a real hassle.

Commonwealth Edison claimed an overdue electric bill for Carson Field that had added up over the years to almost fifty thousand dollars. They demanded full payment before turning the power back on. The Board of Education claimed the property now fell under the auspices of the Parks Department. The parks representative argued that they hadn't monitored the lights for years, so any past due bill was the Board of Ed's responsibility. The Near North Little League certainly didn't have that kind of money. Yet without lights, I saw no way to make the thing work.

With opening day fast approaching and no one willing to budge, I appealed again to Jesse White's political clout. I never did learn what strings he pulled, but one of them turned on the lights. And kept them on. Just in time for the start of our season.

I went to Jesse's office to thank him profusely. I presented him with a leather Bible on which we had embossed his name in gold letters. Tears welled up in his eyes as he read the inscription inside: "The State Representative said, 'Let there be light.' And there was light. Thanks for your support of the neighborhood."

In addition to logistics, I had more than a few interpersonal and public relations issues to smooth over. The press certainly didn't help us on that score.

A number of volunteers were more than a little irritated by a May 1 *Chicago Tribune* piece that came out just before the season started. The primarily positive article, titled "Corporate Types Go to Bat for Ghetto Youngsters," focused on the unique aspects of the league. A cooperative effort between downtown white business executives and neighborhood activists to help black kids. The Cabrini setting. And the interesting team names reflecting both corporate sponsorship and the African heritage of the players: CRT Zulu, Morgan Stanley Mau Mau, Merrill Lynch Watusi, and Northern Trust Maasai.

But about the "cooperative effort" idea, the article said:

> Despite this, doubt still emanates from the league's president, who happens to be [Al] Carter.
>
> "My answer to them [the volunteers] is, 'You manage your blue chip companies downtown,'" says Carter, "'. . . these are impoverished people you are dealing with. It might be good to take your picture with a little black boy and run back downtown and show it to your CEO. But it doesn't mean anything unless it becomes a long-term thing.'
>
> "I appreciate all that has been done. Everybody is sincere and dedicated, but if guys are looking for their halo, they ain't going to get it from me."

Several of our coaches took offense. They felt not only that Al was unappreciative of what they were doing but that he was criticizing them and their motives.

I tried to get the volunteers to understand Al's perspective as someone who'd been working in Cabrini for years and had seen a lot of well-meaning outsiders come and go. At the same time, I tried to convince Al to tone down his skepticism and realize how his comments came across as criticism to our volunteers. Personally, I had developed a friendship with Al and couldn't have cared less what the press said at that point.

Despite the administrative headaches, the leadership responsibilities, and the interpersonal challenges of establishing the league, I found coaching my true calling and great joy. It reaffirmed in my mind how much I loved working with kids.

All the frustrations and trials were more than made up for the evening I handed out the uniforms at the end of practice. Just watching those kids' eyes light up as they all tried on their new jerseys and caps was worth every bit of effort. And we hadn't even played our first game yet.

The real fun began when we opened our season the first week of June. Once the games of summer started, the Near North Little League looked and sounded a lot like youth baseball anywhere. Cheers and tears. Winners and losers. Men and boys together enjoying America's favorite pastime. I was amazed how much time and energy and organization it all required.

To be honest, when you're coaching your own team *and* calling the game behind the plate because the umpire didn't show, and it's ninety-five degrees in July, you don't always have fun. You have to remind yourself why you're out there. But you do what you have to do.

Home-plate umps in the inner city deserve combat pay. Often when a catcher disagrees with your strike zone, he's apt to call time and go talk to his pitcher. When he comes back, he'll start missing pitches on purpose and you get pummeled back there.

I remember one day when I was stuck with the dual role of coach and ump. The opposing team's catcher naturally thought me biased. He was a left-hander wearing a regular catcher's mitt on the wrong hand, which tells you all you need to know about his scrappy personality. *You gotta like that.* He was talkin' to every hitter. Finally, it was "Casey at the Bat" time—bottom of the sixth, the score 4-1, two outs, bases loaded, and my team's last batter came to the plate.

He hit a hard grounder to short. Easy play. Force at second. Game over, right?

But this is Little League. The shortstop misplayed the ball, which rolled into left center. With two down, everyone was running on contact. So by the time the left fielder chased down the ball, three runners had already crossed the plate and the batter was rounding third and heading home.

Grand slam! *E-6, if you're scoring at home.*

The catcher hurled his mitt down in disgust just as the relay man cut loose with his throw. The baseball nailed the poor catcher just above the eye, and a big bloody welt ballooned up. He wasn't one of my players, he was on the other team, but I was the ump and the vice president of the league. Plus I had a car. So I was the one who took this boy to the trauma center at Northwestern Hospital just a few blocks away.

An ER nurse applied ice and said she thought he was going to be fine, but she wanted him to see a doctor because it was a pretty nasty welt. We'd been there an hour by that time, so I said, "There's a McDonald's right around the corner. While we're waiting for the doc, why don't I run out and get us both something to eat?"

The kid's eyes lit up. "That sounds great," he said with a grin. *He's my best buddy now, right.*

So I walked to McDonald's to buy burgers, fries, and cokes. When I returned maybe twelve minutes later, he wasn't there. He was inside now, in the exam area with all the curtains. So I went searching for him. When I finally found the right curtain and walked up beside the bed, he looked up, surprised, and said, "You came back!" *Like he can't believe it.* "You came back!"

Then it hit me! When I walked out of that ER to run to McDonald's, even though I said I'd be right back, he figured I'd bolted on him. He didn't expect ever to see me again. He'd already known too many adults who had walked out of his life and never came back.

My nine-to-twelve-year-olds Pygmy team won the regular season title but lost to the Ewes in our postseason playoffs. Don't worry. We hadn't expected to make the Little League World Series in Williamsport our first year. So I was thrilled when the Near North All Stars actually won a game in the first round of our district tournament.

A lot of people took notice of what happened on our corner across from Cabrini-Green that summer of 1991. We never solicited publicity, but both CNN and *ABC Evening News* sent camera crews and ran stories about the league. As much as I tried to steer the reporters to Al Carter and some of the other African-American coaches, the stories all took the same angle—white business executives help black children in poor neighborhood. So I always had mixed feelings about the news coverage, as I did when I was surprised and honored to be named the State of Illinois' Little League Volunteer of the Year at the end of the season and when the league received one of President Bush's Points of Light awards later that year.

I knew that neither first-year awards nor national news coverage could ever be a true measure of Near North's success. Our greatest achievements would be seen in the ongoing impact the experience had on the lives of those involved in our league.

I think of my friend Paul O'Connor. I knew him as a fraternity brother and rugby teammate from our time together at Columbia. So when I'd been desperate to find coaches at the beginning of the year, I called Paul right away. At the outset of our conversation, I naturally asked how he and his wife, Holly, were doing.

"Not so good," he joked. "She just left me." Paul would always say that about Holly, worried she would wake up one day and leave him.

Being my usual sensitive self, I tried to match his attempted casual tone by saying, "Great, great. Then you've got plenty of time now, pal. So how's about coachin' a team in this Little League we're just startin' ..."

Paul agreed to become head coach of the Lincoln Park Physical Therapy Zulus. And it was after a night game midway through the season, when I noticed Holly drive up with pizza for the whole Zulu team. By the end of the season, Holly was coaching first base and keeping Paul's scorebook.

I had never considered the positive impact our Little League experience could have on all of our relationships when I asked Paul to coach. And there's absolutely no way I could have imagined everything that happened in the O'Connors' lives as a result. Not only do they continue to coach ten years later, but on their fifteenth anniversary, it was my privilege to stand with them in St. Paul's Chapel on the Columbia University campus to renew their wedding vows in a moving ceremony that included Bible readings by Miles and Joe—just two of several African-American Little Leaguers Paul and Holly have coached and then taken in over the years.

But the best measure of the league's success isn't even what happened in the lives of so many volunteers. For me the greatest sense of satisfaction comes from the reactions of the kids themselves. No sooner had we held our big season-ending awards banquet at a local church than I began to receive phone calls asking, "Hey, Coach Bob. What we doin' next week?"

CLOSE CALLS

Our players weren't the only ones sorry to see our season wind down. Many of our league's volunteers were just as unhappy to see their player-coach relationships end. So we didn't end them.

A lot of us continued to gather our teams for regular off-season recreation. We held cookouts and parties. I took some of my players to local high school and college football or basketball games.

We'd actually have our own nerf football games in the stands during Northwestern games in the early '90s before the Wildcats started winning. Coach Gary Barnett even allowed our Little League guys to attend practices and share training table meals with his team.

Much informal mentoring took place, and out of that grew some more-structured tutoring opportunities. A number of coaches even helped provide tuition to get some of the struggling kids into a stronger educational environment in local Catholic schools. Tina and I sponsored two families at St. Joseph School.

In "real life," my insurance business flourished. With so much of the firm's new business back in New York, Tina and I had begun the year seriously thinking about returning to the Big Apple. Now we saw the success of the league and all the relationships developing there as part of God's direction that we should stay in Chicago, even if that meant downsizing or limiting the business. There were just too many good and growing things happening that overrode business or monetary priorities.

However, we didn't think we needed to stay in the house we were living in. Because our SoNo neighborhood was rapidly changing. For the "better."

Our desire all along was to live in a low-income area where we could reach out to serve those around us. So the steady gentrification of our street, and the increased cost of property in our area, prompted us to seriously consider a move to a larger place with room for our growing family—and more.

When we saw a newspaper ad for a brand-new construction company offering to design and build a home on the city's West Side—twice the house for half the price we would have to pay in our neighborhood—we jumped at the deal. We built a four-story greystone with the ground floor designed to serve as a halfway house for anyone in need. As Christians, the fact that our home would be in an older, run-down, low-income city neighborhood was a plus in our minds. Why would we move where we'd be surrounded by other rich white people simply because we could afford to?

In fact, less than a block away from our new home, we found and helped pay for a place for the family of one of my players to move in—out of the projects. Despite moving to the West Side, we weren't going to walk away from Cabrini-Green, the league, or any of the relationships we now had with the players, families, and coaches we'd encountered there.

I learned through experience that the Cabrini neighborhood had a history of "white help" that had quickly come and gone. A few years earlier, the husband of former Chicago Mayor Jane Byrne had even started, during his wife's administration, a good but short-lived Little League program for Cabrini-Green kids. So when people asked me if I was running for some office, I realized the reason for cynicism and suspicion in so many poor neighborhoods: people, black or white, rarely do anything there without some ulterior motive.

It took a while to convince some people we had no personal agenda, that we were simply motivated by faith to help neighborhood kids grow by linking them up with other caring, and reliable business men and women—our unbelievably dedicated volunteers. Many of whom became my closest friends in the process. Practically all of these volunteers, both black and white, in time proved that they too had no political or financial intentions.

Fortunately, all but a handful of our coaches re-upped for a second season, and we had a bunch of new volunteers. We needed all the help we could get to run a league that had expanded to twenty-eight teams serving more than four hundred kids.

Unfortunately, some familiar tensions were resurrected by more media coverage we never sought and frankly could have done without. One of the assistant coaches for the Kikuyus sold an article about our league's first season to *Sports Illustrated*. We would find out later that he parlayed that article into a publishing contract with an advance to write a book about the Near North Little League's second season.

The *SI* article, pretty much parroting all the prior media coverage, hooked readers by focusing on the idea of white corporate executives volunteering to run a baseball league for underprivileged black kids in a notoriously tough inner-city neighborhood, completely ignoring the fact that many of the "downtown executives" serving as volunteer coaches in our program were African-American—Greg White, Tony Hawthorne, Greg Johnson, Sean Armstead, Jim Reynolds, Kristi Dinkins, Charles Hudson, Alan Eaton, and others.

The magazine article also resurrected the controversy (using almost exactly the same words) the *Tribune* had triggered the previous year by quoting Al Carter again saying, "Sure a lot of coaches showed up, but a lot of them came for the glamour. People look at it as if white America is the savior of all our problems. With them, there will be no more fighting, no more shooting, no more problems at all. Besides [coaching] is a nice way to get a halo from your CEO back downtown."

I thought that was classic journalism, hyping the negative. Some of our coaches were mad again. And once more it was left to me to smooth things over. Fortunately, we could rely on our commissioner, Greg White, a twenty-eight-year-old African-American real-estate banker and Harvard Business School grad whose organizational and communication skills helped insulate the coaches from the printed skepticism.

By the start of the 1992 season, the Near North Little League had expanded and now included a small girl's softball division. We had begun awarding some scholarships to send players to private school, scheduled road trips and a camp experience for the teams, and had seen many wonderful relationships forged between people who never would have met if not for our league. The Near North Little League had new official banners to hang at Carson Field, and we published a newsletter for the families of coaches and players. We also created a brochure describing the Near North Little League and its mission.

But any organizational hassles and tensions created by the press soon seemed pretty insignificant compared with other conflicts going on in the neighborhood that summer.

A number of our players got beaten up on their way home from Carson Field. So more and more coaches began picking up and dropping off kids for games and practices. For whatever reason, gang violence had intensified to the point that you'd hear gunfire almost every night as one side or the other showed off their arsenal.

I remember during one night game I heard the *ping, ping, ping* of bullets ricocheting off the El tracks just behind our dugout. All of our players instinctively hit the ground. Except one. My right fielder, a middle-class African-American kid who lived over on North Avenue, was still standing in his position without a clue as to why all his streetwise teammates were suddenly lying in the grass. I yelled, "Halston!" and waved him down. But he still didn't understand. So I jumped to my feet, raced into the outfield, pulled him low, and ran with him into the infield, where everyone was now scampering to the cars parked along the street for cover. We resumed the game when the shooting stopped a few minutes later. But the next inning, umpire Bill Seitz ran over from the other diamond and said, "Forget it, Bob. I'm still hearin' bullets whizzin' by!" So we called the games and sent everyone home for the evening.

Unfortunately, home wasn't exactly a safe haven for a lot of our Near North players.

Dionte, my second baseman, was usually an hour early for games—a real field rat like I used to be. That's why I was perturbed one Saturday morning at five minutes to eleven when there was still no sign of him. We had a great coaching staff for the Pygmy that year—Mike Edwards, who had pitched in college for Valparaiso, along with Bill Vranos and Willie Naugles again. They finished warm-ups with the kids as I jumped in my station wagon to go find Dionte.

One of the good things about the Near North Little League was that all of our players lived within ten blocks of the field. So I didn't have far to go.

I went through the usual hassle entering 502 West Oak. The city had really beefed up security as a result of recent shootings. A guard checked my photo ID against some list. Then he reluctantly buzzed me in, even though he had seen me twenty times.

It was almost game time, so I took the stairs two at a time. I rapped at the apartment door five times. Inside I heard shouting. The TV and the stereo played simultaneously. The door opened six inches, the extent of the chain. In the crack, I could see half of a woman's dark face—makeup smeared, one bloodshot eye. Behind her, a wasted white guy in his underwear sat on a tattered couch, smoking and nursing a forty-two-ounce Olde English Beer bottle. In front of him on a dirty glass coffee table were two sparkling lines of white powder and a razor blade.

Leaning against the bedroom doorjamb at the far end of the apartment was my leadoff hitter in his uniform, glove in hand, tears rolling down his cheeks. *Been a long night.*

"Hi, Ms. Johnson," I offered in cheerful greeting. "Big play-off game today," I said, wedging my foot in the doorway. The guy on the couch looked at my foot uneasily.

"He punished, Coach. Dionte got a real smart mouth on him," she told me.

The guy swore and said, "Let da kid go ta his ballgame, May. Den you and me can have some peace and quiet and watch dis next movie."

"C'mon then, Dionte," she relented. "Go to your stupid game. But I'll deal witchu when you get home!"

The instant his mother released the chain, Dionte slipped past her. His five-year-old brother, Terrell, dressed only in shorts and sneakers, squeezed out into the hall right behind him. The three of us scooted down the dank, urine-scented stairwell, hurried out the door, and jumped in the car.

There was a forty-dollar traffic ticket on my windshield. No parking.

Game time.

The Near North Little League not only helped get kids out of the house; we got a lot of them out of the neighborhood. Way out. At least for a little while.

I'd been shocked during our first season to learn just what isolated lives many of the kids in Cabrini-Green lived. One stifling hot day, after a long sweaty practice, I piled the kids into my station wagon and drove over to the lakeshore for a refreshing dip. I couldn't believe it when several of the boys told me it was the first time they'd ever seen Lake Michigan or been to any of the magnificent shoreline parks just a half-dozen city blocks from where they'd lived all their lives. We made postpractice beach trips a regular event after that.

And taking my team to Iowa after our inaugural season had been such a huge adventure and positive experience for Brian Dixon and his teammates that I worked out a special deal with an old friend of B. J.'s at a Christian foundation in Dubuque called Four Mounds to bring several of our teams out the following year. We built the cost into the price of sponsoring a team and mapped out a league schedule that gave each team that could go a different break sometime during the season. In Iowa our teams would play exhibition games with area Little League teams and then camp out in the woods at night.

There's nothin' like the hardship of camping adventures to bond teammates together. Many volunteers told me the trip was a highlight of their whole coaching experience. It gave them meaningful time with the kids as well as allowing everyone a welcome respite from the unrelenting pressures of city life.

I told people we were trading the sounds of sirens and bullets for silence and crickets. Crickets make me nervous, but I could get used to them.

The rest of that year seemed to offer constant notice that we weren't in Iowa anymore. One harsh reminder about the reality of city life took place as the '92 playoffs began.

Even after we moved to the West Side, we still stored some of our baseball equipment in the garage of our old house just four blocks from Carson Field. So when one of the coaches requested extra practice balls, Tina drove by the garage late one afternoon planning to get the balls and drop them off at the field during that evening's games.

Tina, who was seven months pregnant with our third child, drove past the stable, turned down the alley under the El tracks, and pulled right into the garage. She left the car there and closed the garage door while she walked next door to say hello to our old neighbors. No one was home, so she hurried back to the garage to get the baseballs and leave.

Intent on unlocking the side door to the garage with her key, Tina didn't hear any footsteps. She never knew anyone was there until a powerful man grabbed her from behind and shoved her into the darkened garage. When he closed the door behind them, Tina tried to jerk away and escape in the blackness. But there wasn't much room between the garage wall and our car, so she really had nowhere to go. As they struggled, her attacker yanked open the car's passenger door and shoved her into the car.

Our auto alarm was designed to go off if you open the passenger side first. So it did.

And it was loud. When her incensed attacker paused in surprise, Tina had the presence of mind to reach up and press the garage-door opener clipped on the driver's-side visor.

With the car alarm still blasting and the garage door now suddenly swinging open and letting daylight in, the attacker let go of Tina and fled. She caught her only glimpse of him through the rear window of the car—the back of a large man wearing red winter gloves—as he ran out of the garage and down the alley.

It could have been worse.

Tina was shaken. We both were.

Random bullets ricocheting off the El track were one thing. But it's a whole different ballgame when somebody goes after your pregnant wife. This attack on Tina seemed ominously personal. I thought, *Maybe it's time for me to give up this crazy dream and walk away.* It just didn't seem worth it anymore.

"Look at all the great things that are going on through the league," Tina argued. "We can't leave now."

I knew she was right. But I was still awfully steamed as the Pygmy players took the field for our playoff game that Saturday. Even though Tina insisted I coach, my team might have been better off without me. We were eliminated from the playoffs by a team we should have beaten.

Two months later, in October of 1992, our son Isaiah was born at the same time another act of violence in our neighborhood claimed an innocent life and made national headlines.

BULLETS

Tina and I read the October 14 *Chicago Tribune*'s front-page report sitting on her hospital bed the following morning.

It usually took Dantrell Davis about a minute to walk across the cracked blacktop that separated his Cabrini-Green high-rise from his school. Yet every step of that short journey was filled with danger, just as every minute of a child's day in the Near North public housing project holds the threat of violence. The smallest and most innocent of Cabrini residents are not safe.

On Tuesday morning, as Dantrell started toward the Jenner School, yellow-jacketed members of the Cabrini parent patrol stood watch to fend off trouble. At the school door, teachers waited to shepherd children inside, more concerned with safety than tardiness.

Two police officers were stationed at a nearby corner. . . . As a final precautionary measure, Dantrell's mother, Annette Freeman, accompanied the 7-year-old boy on the short walk across the lot.

Dantrell never made it 10 feet. Moments after the 9 a.m. school bell rang, a single rifle shot was fired. It struck Dantrell in the head.

His mother crouched over the small body, screaming. "Please baby, don't die. Please come and get my baby. Please hurry," Ray Baker, a teacher who witnessed the shooting, recounted.

Half an hour later, Dantrell was pronounced dead at Children's Memorial Hospital. He was the third child from the school killed this year.

Not only were Chicagoans horrified by this slaying, but the story made national headlines, became symbolic of the failure of public housing across the country, and became a topic for discussion in the next presidential debate. But an even bigger shock for me came when I picked up the October 15 *Tribune* and read a front-page article reporting more heartbreaking news.

A 33-year-old man with a record of weapons offenses was charged Wednesday with the sniper slaying of a Cabrini-Green child whose death has sparked calls for National Guard intervention and refocused attention on Chicago's blighted public housing.

Anthony Garrett, an alleged gang leader, was charged with murder for the shooting of Dantrell Davis, 7, who died from a single gunshot wound to the face outside 502 W. Oak St. as he began a 100-foot walk to school Tuesday morning, police said.

The boy was the latest casualty of an ongoing turf war for control of the high-rise buildings at the Cabrini-Green public housing complex, according to police. Police arrested Garrett about noon Wednesday after learning his nickname from residents in the housing complex. Although he first denied shooting the boy, Garrett confessed to the crime saying "his conscience was bothering him," said Belmont Area Cmdr. William Callaghan.

I knew Anthony Garrett! Al Carter had recruited him to umpire some of our Near North Little League games. I'd known Junebug (his street name) had the same problem I'd had with booze. So I'd taken him with me to the Mustard Seed a few times. After he'd said he wanted to give the program a try, I'd talked to a friend of mine who secured Anthony an entry-level job in the laundry of a large health club just a few blocks from Cabrini-Green. Last time I'd seen him, I'd thought he was doing fine, but I called my friend at the health club, who told me Anthony hadn't been working there for the past several weeks. "Took off sick a couple days claiming he'd gotten soap in his eyes. Never came back."

It didn't take the media long to identify Garrett as "an umpire for Cabrini children in the local Near North Little League" and to quote Al: "'I needed him out there because of his influence with young people and because of his knowledge of the turf wars (in Cabrini),' said Carter, an area manager in the anti-gang Chicago Intervention Network. 'They looked up to him because he was an adult black man. Anthony was there not just to umpire but to try to steer these young people away from the fighting.'"

The question I had, and which none of the articles answered, was why. Based on his initial confession, police thought Garrett had been shooting at members of a rival gang and accidentally hit the boy. When Garrett later recanted that confession and it was learned the boy's mother was the niece of a major Chicago gang leader, there was speculation that the shooting was intentional and motivated by revenge. Later still, I heard talk around the neighborhood saying Garrett hadn't done the shooting, that he was framed or was taking the fall for someone else. All I knew for sure was that Anthony Garrett was convicted and sentenced to one hundred years in prison, and that another innocent child died in a senseless tragedy and the league got a little more undeserved negative publicity.

The following spring, I felt ready to give up my formal leadership role in the league. While I planned to sponsor and continue working with the families and coaches I now had friendships with,

I really wanted to focus more of my energies on my growing family. But many of the coaches approached me saying I should help solidify the Near North Little League at least one more season, even though it was no longer our neighborhood.

I finally agreed. And in our organization's first election ever, I was elected president of the Near North Little League for 1993. Believe me, I did not want the job. I voted for Al. But he wasn't around as much that second season. Twenty-eight of the other twenty-nine head coaches voted for me. So I took the reins of the league, determined to leave it stronger and in good hands at the end of my term.

One of my first challenges at the beginning of that 1993 season was dealing with the fallout from the assistant coach's book. I received several anonymous threatening phone calls at home and at work. And on the field, I was personally lambasted by self-appointed Cabrini spokesperson-activist Marion "Queen Nzinga" Stamps. God rest her soul. Believe me, when Mrs. Stamps finished cursing you out, you knew you were white.

Most of the book was accurate. But some of it wasn't.

The writer mentioned me by name over one hundred times and inaccurately told my AA story without my permission. After I told him directly that I didn't want my personal story to appear in the book, he included it anyway.

He also made little attempt to accurately portray any spiritual motivation behind the volunteer effort so many people had put into the league. In places, the author seemed to mock our faith without ever acknowledging the obvious truth: without that faith, there would be no Near North Little League to write articles or books about.

A number of friends, including several of our African-American coaches were angry. Commissioner Greg White, a dear friend who is still coaching today, told me, "I can't believe he did that. Shouldn't we do something?"

But the book came off the presses right about the time of Brian Dixon's death. And my twelve-year-old shortstop had just moved into our loft to escape some serious family problems. So I had plenty of other concerns to think about. That helped me keep things in perspective and decide to just forget about the author and to let what he said in his book go.

That was even before he left an autographed copy of the book with my receptionist. I laughed when I read the inscription. "To Bob, one of the most amazing men I've ever met. Keep it up."

I laughed again later when I told Al Carter about it. "That cat didn't even give me a copy," Al told me.

We both laughed at that.

Later we heard that the author had sold the movie rights to his book to Paramount Pictures for a very sizable sum—half up front and the other half when and if the movie ever got made. We also heard that Paramount had sent a camera crew on the Kikuyus Iowa trip and that the studio had compensated the author and some of the other Kikuyu coaches for that. But the Little League never received a penny for that either.

Some of our league volunteers were incensed and wanted me to confront the writer. But he wasn't around as much that season. And later when I heard he'd moved back to Alaska, I thought that would be the last I'd ever hear about him, the book, and all this talk about a Hollywood movie.

Despite the controversies and the heartbreak we encountered that year, the 1993 season seemed to come off with fewer volunteer problems to solve. Even with my increased responsibilities as league president, I encountered a lot less administrative headaches than I did the first two years.

Though there were the usual challenges of coaching and dealing with families, parents, and kids. And some outright insanity.

Twelve-year-old boys can be brutal with one another. Our center fielder that year was a particularly boisterous dispenser of verbal abuse. Rocket constantly taunted our chunky players.

"Ol' boy be so fat his clothes say Goodyear on 'em."

"Maa-an, where you get those Santa Claus pants?"

When Rocket's victims got mad, he'd laugh it off. "Didn't mean nuthin' by it. Just raggin' you, man." Like he couldn't imagine why anyone wanted to make a big deal of it.

Midway through the season, however, I noticed Rocket seemed uncharacteristically morose. The week before we left to play in Iowa, he showed up for practice with his hair "jeri-curled.'"

That was it. Revenge of the fat boys.

"Look, isn't that Shirley Temple?"

"Hey Prince, sing one for us."

Or worse, they'd just look down the bench, pretend to whisper, then giggle. Before long, Rocket started crying. I had no idea what was going on, but I immediately declared a moratorium on all verbal flak. And the ceasefire held for a day or two.

But on the first night of the road trip, he caught more abuse than ever after one of his teammates pointed out the dark stains on the back of Rocket's white baseball pants. When the taunts soon erupted into a fistfight, our camp counselor, Sam Dillon, pulled Rocket aside and tried to talk with the boy.

The last night of our trip, after the bonfire burned down and the boys headed for bed, Sam motioned me off to the side and said, "We gotta talk, Bob!"

"What about?" I wanted to know.

"About Rocket."

Earlier that evening, when they were walking by themselves, Rocket tearfully confessed to Sam, "My mother's boyfriend be doin' stuff to me. Then she and him done this to my hair, man, when they be all high and stuff."

I really thought nothing could faze me anymore. Not after everything I'd done. Not after some of the bizarre "adult" behavior I'd seen at after-hours clubs in New York years ago.

But that was a world away. This was Little League.

Nothing like this is your fault when you're eleven.

I didn't get much sleep that night. And I thought about Rocket the entire drive home the next afternoon. *Could he be making the story up? How could any mother smoke crack and watch her boyfriend sodomize her son?* I didn't want to think it could happen. But when it came right down to it, I did believe it. And I felt a responsibility to help this boy. To stop this abuse. *But how? I need to report it. And what will happen then?* I didn't know what to do.

We'd all had a great trip. But I was physically and emotionally exhausted by the time we got back to Chicago. Rocket rode shotgun as we let off the last of the other players late that Sunday night. He sat straight up in the seat, his hands tightly gripping the armrests. It wasn't difficult to tell he didn't want to be home.

I thought about confronting the issue directly when I dropped Rocket off. *I have to do something! But what will his mom and her boyfriend do to him if they know he told?*

When I pulled into the parking lot, there were dozens of people hanging out there trying to beat the July heat. Several cranked-up stereos and stand-alone boom boxes blasted music from open car trunks. Rocket's mom was there partying, so she walked over to greet the van. The man with her wore dangling earrings and his own jeri curls.

What could I do? I had no proof. That was this boy's mother. I was just his coach.

My heart was pumpin' as I entertained thoughts of jackin' this guy up, right then and there. It would have been so easy. *Just grab both earrings and headbutt 'im full blast. But I don't even know if he's the guy.*

His mother slurred at me, "Thhhank you, Coach Bob. You real. I mmmmean, you are really real."

"Rocket played great all week," I told her. "You'd be real proud of him. Can you come to practice tomorrow?" *Maybe I could decide what to do by then?*

"What fo'?"

"It would be great for you to see how well he's doing," I replied. *Maybe I could talk to her alone there.*

"We'll see," she said with no real conviction. "Good night, now."

And that was it. I watched Rocket walk away between them. Twice he looked back and waved weakly before he faded into the giant shadow of his building.

I told Tina about Rocket as soon as I got home. I prayed in earnest that night with her and again during my morning run to the office. At practice that Monday afternoon, a barrel-chested man in a maintenance uniform sat silently on the sidelines and watched us go through our drills. Afterward, he introduced himself as Rocket's father. And he told me, "My boy will be livin' with me now."

I breathed a sigh of relief. *Thank you, Lord.*

Rocket played well that Saturday as his father watched proudly. Although we still had a few more games to play, the boy was a no-show for the next game the following week. When I called, I got a recording saying the phone number I had for him "has been disconnected." I never saw Rocket again. I could only hope and pray he and his father got a fresh start somewhere else.

During the 1991 and 1992 seasons, we'd signed up our eleven-to-twelve-year-old Near North All Stars to compete for a shot at the Little League World Series in Williamsport, Pennsylvania. That's when we learned that youth baseball can get a little serious.

Baseball is a learned-skill sport. And most of our players were relatively new to the game. So those first couple of years, we got knocked out in the first round, via the ten-run slaughter rule, by well-drilled suburban teams.

By the 1993 season, however, we were competitive enough to win a few postseason games. Two of the four all-star coaches— Mike Edwards and Willie Naugles Sr.—had helped me for years with my Pygmy teams. Willie Jr. and Timmy Barnes from our team played on the squad. So I drove out to the burbs after work to cheer for my guys. Both teams were 2-1 going into the game. So the pressure was on, knowing the loser would be knocked out of the double-elimination tournament.

We fell behind early, 4-0. In the bottom of the fourth, Willie Naugles Jr., who was built like a miniature Kirby Puckett, blasted a towering homer to pull us within two. When we came to bat for our last licks two innings later, the score remained 4-2. Rain threatened to end the game early as thunder rumbled in the distance, the sky grew dark, and bright lights illuminated the nicest field our boys had ever played on.

Our number-nine hitter bunted his way on, and Timmy followed with a base hit. But our next two hitters lined out. Runners on first and second, two down, Willie up, his father (one of only three of my players' dads I'd met in three seasons) coaching third.

Willie lined a base hit to center and their outfielder instinctively threw home. Our lead runner evaded the tag by leaping over the catcher kneeling to block the plate and raced into our jubilant dugout. It was 4-3 now.

But the opposition's coaches were screaming at the umpire, "He missed home!" and foolishly encouraging their catcher to go find the runner and tag him. The catcher ran to our dugout and in the melee of happy black faces couldn't figure out who to tag. *And we're not helpin'.*

Meanwhile, Willie Naugles Sr. down in the third-base coach's box was frantically waving Timmy and Willie Jr. on around the bases. Both boys scored. And the Near North All Stars won the game 5-4.

The moment Willie Jr.'s foot hit home plate, the sky opened up. As the rain poured down on them, our boys lined up for the ceremonial handshake. The shoe was on the other foot this time.

There was no joy in Mudville that night. Helmets were flyin' and parents were holdin' back the other team's coach to keep him from attacking the umpire.

My suit was drenched from the downpour when we entered a nearby Italian restaurant to celebrate. Mike Koldyke, a venture capitalist and head of the Chicago School Finance Authority, who sponsored one of the teams in our league, treated all the players and fans to a feast. Mike and Willie Naugles raised their glasses together in a toast and "thanks for holdin' the rain."

"This league is the best thing that ever happened to me'n Boo," Willie told me, looking proudly at his son.

That'll keep you comin' back.

OUTSIDE THE LINES

That restaurant celebration was just one of a thousand affirming moments we witnessed through Little League. Our vision from the outset was for Near North to become an environment in which positive relationships could develop between coaches and players—and both their families.

The poorest urban people I encountered—struggling families living in welfare hotels and government housing projects or the most destitute street people wandering into AA meetings in search of a safe place to sit—often felt disconnected from vital resources that could offer any means, or even hope, for improvement. The shame is that great resources are often only a few blocks away.

My Christian friends at the Lamb's Church in New York and Father William in Bolivia had shown me that the most effective way to connect needy people with resources that can help is through personal relationships. These can be developed naturally by living among the people who need the help. This is why I became convinced that what under-resourced children and families of Chicago (or Harlem or Watts or wherever) needed most was not another well-intentioned government program but a connected neighbor. In our case, that neighbor could even be a baseball coach.

While I hadn't hit upon the baseball strategy right away, I'd tested the personal connection theory many times by helping get guys into rehabilitation programs if they were "sick and tired of being sick and tired." I'd also helped some of those guys get jobs.

In the process, I learned there is often a fine line between enabling someone and helping them seize their opportunity to make a better life. Almost everyone says they want a better life. Some rise to the challenge. Others don't.

After living in Chicago for a while, I had volunteered through LaSalle Street Church to work in a program called Cabrini Alive. While I'm sure this service ministry did good things for some people, my assignment was scraping and painting a government-subsidized apartment while the obese tenant, who was about my age, sat on the couch eating potato chips, drinking Coca-Cola, and watching TV. When she asked me to move so she could see the screen, I felt like walking out. Instead, I finished my assignment, vowing never to do anything like that again. But I was more determined than ever to find a means of being a neighbor who could connect people with resources they not only needed but could be held accountable for.

The Little League grew out of that concern.

As a "connected" coach, I often heard the operator's phrase "has been disconnected" when I called my players. Things sounded a little more hopeful when I heard that a phone "has been *temporarily* disconnected." The broader issue of disconnectedness is something no one talks about. It's the pink elephant in the living room that no one dares mention, yet it's at the heart of so many urban issues.

The man begging on the bridge by Union Station doesn't need "some change." He needs sobriety, a job, and accountability to the person who got him that job.

The poor black teenager living with a single parent doesn't just need to graduate from high school; he needs a completed financial aid form, a plane ticket, the first semester's rent, and accountability to the person who helped him. This might make some people uncomfortable, but Irish guys still help Irish kids, just like Jewish guys help Jewish kids. But the old message we give inner-city kids, "If you make it, you can get out," has indeed "worked." Too many who have made it got out . . . and stayed out. So some of the rest of us need to pitch in.

Making those connections takes time and effort. And yes, you might "get used" from time to time. But it's not like getting nailed to a cross.

In its first three years, Near North proved to me that connections change lives. The league's informal scholarship program had practically taken off on its own. Some of the other coaches took that ball and ran with it. Where we'd provided a dozen scholarships after the first year, more coaches kicked in during the following years and channeled their funds into Highsight, a new mentor-scholarship program a local attorney had founded for nearby St. Joseph Catholic School. By 1993, Near North coaches paid the private-parochial school admission for dozens of our league's most promising students. Many of them also assisted in an after-school tutoring program through which additional mentoring opportunities developed. Players' families developed close friendships with coaches and their families. Coaches were finding jobs for the parents of their players. And some volunteers had taken kids into their homes as unofficial and in some cases official foster children.

In 1993, a South Side pastor invited us to start another baseball program. Greg White, using the experience he'd gained as commissioner of Near North, helped me spearhead the new Englewood community Little League on Chicago's South Side that spring. We sought permission to use the ball diamonds at Englewood High School and held most of our organizational meetings at the Antioch Missionary Baptist Church across the street from the fields.

In Cabrini, some community leaders had acted as if we needed their permission to help the kids in the Little League. We felt the only permission needed to help a child came from a parent or guardian. Those same community leaders seemed to resent anyone helping "their youth" without their involvement or sometimes without their sharing in some financial gain. Indeed, as the Near North Little League grew, other organizations wanted to get in on "the action." Even a local Parks District official wanting "to use our numbers" called and asked for an address and phone list of all the players.

We experienced none of that competition on the South Side. From the beginning, everyone in Englewood seemed glad to have us there.

This made me wonder what was going on the first day of sign-ups when I arrived at the field to find hardly anyone there. *What happened? Did we offend someone?* We'd advertised heavily in the community and passed out flyers in all the nearby schools, announcing the formation of the league and promoting a big lead-off event that would include another instructional clinic conducted by Christian professional ballplayers. We'd expected a big crowd.

The pros showed a few minutes ahead of schedule to do their setup. But still only a handful of kids.

Finally, about five minutes before the program was supposed to start, a long line of cars wheeled around the corner and cruised into the parking lot. More than forty vehicles in all. When the doors opened, one hundred and fifty kids piled out.

Their blue and black colors made it easy to tell the drivers were all Gangster Disciples. The troops hung around to watch the clinic and to listen to a couple of the athletes share their spiritual testimonies afterward. They made sure the kids behaved and picked up all the necessary registration forms. And when the event ended, the GDs herded all the kids back into their cars and drove them home.

The Englewood Little League started sweet with a dozen teams of ten-to-twelve-year-olds that first year. As always, the neighborhood kids were raring to go, eager to be a part of something that actually happened as advertised. Our biggest challenge in making it happen was staffing. Located on Chicago's South Side, almost ten miles from the Loop, we had a much tougher time getting volunteers from the downtown business community. So most of that league's coaches were drawn from the neighborhood.

We tried to work with what we had.

For a few weeks, these men did a pretty good job of working with kids on the field. Off the field, I knew some of our coaches weren't what you would call consistently positive role models.

But adult enthusiasm for the league waned the following year. Coaches quit and a few teams folded. Some equipment was picked up and never seen again, which hadn't been a serious problem in the Near North Little League. We just didn't find enough consistent community leadership for the league in Englewood at the time. The Gangster Disciples were all for us, but you can't sell drugs on Friday night and coach Little League the next morning. That's obviously not the kind of connection kids need—or that we wanted to provide. So after the second season, we handed the program and equipment over to Englewood High School and concentrated our energies in other directions.

During those early Little League years, I never quit trying to connect with individuals I encountered in other relationships. I met Galen C. one morning at the Mustard Seed. As the meeting wound down, I asked, "Anyone here today have any burning desires?" This handsome twenty-six-year-old man raised his hand and said he'd just gotten out of drug treatment. While he'd been on drugs, he'd gotten arrested for armed robbery. But through a special program available to those who committed crimes under the influence, the judge sentenced him to rehab. "This is the first time ever I've been out in the world not high. And I'm scared to death out here!"

So I stayed and talked to Galen for a while. He was a nice guy, well spoken. I spoke to his parole officer. We'd recently moved into our house on the West Side, so I invited him to move in as our very first guest.

I also talked to a friend, the business manager of a large downtown firm, who got Galen a maintenance job on the night crew there. Eight bucks an hour, plus all the food he could eat in the company kitchen. Galen was thrilled.

Until his first payday. He brought the check by my office for me to go with him and set up his very first checking account. I expected him to be excited. But when he showed me his check, he was shaking and on the verge of tears. "Look at this!"

I looked. One week's pay. Forty hours. Gross $320, net around $250. "What's wrong with it?" I asked.

He pointed at the deductions. "What's this FICA, FUTA stuff?"

Suddenly it hit me. Galen thought he was being ripped off because he wasn't getting the full $320.

"Galen," I told him, "you know that general assistance you were on for so many years—that GA? This is where it comes from."

"No, man!" Galen said. "I used to get my checks from the government!"

Here he was, a twenty-six-year-old man who had no idea that other people's taxes paid for his welfare. That every working person in the country chips in for those who aren't working. No one had ever explained that to him.

Galen turned out to be an excellent worker. We eventually got him another job. He moved out on his own and has been gainfully employed, paying FICA, and staying out of jail ever since.

I met the "Sandman" when Al Carter called and asked me if I could help "a pretty serious dude" who'd just been released from prison. So I had lunch with Sam, who admitted to me he'd been a gang leader and enforcer who'd served a long term for killing two people in a fight. He also told me about encountering Mother York, an elderly, black woman evangelist who'd had a prison ministry at the Cook County Jail for decades. She'd convinced him not only that he could be loved and forgiven but that God could help him turn his life around and be a different kind of person—even in prison. And he'd done that, even earning his college degree by correspondence during his years of incarceration.

But now Sam realized it was going to be a lot harder living a Christian life on the outside, because he was suddenly back on his turf with no resources or friends apart from his old gang contacts. He wasn't sure if, or how, he could stay straight.

I invited Sam to move into the basement with Galen and helped him get a factory job assembling televisions for Zenith. During the year and a half he lived with us, Sam became a dear friend and served as my resident guru on Chicago gangs. He not only shared interesting experiences from his youth but gave me insight into today's gang mentality and explained some of the background for the conflict still going on around the city. He had little respect for, and wanted nothing to do with, the current gang leaders. Which is one reason he eventually decided he wanted to get away from Chicago, his old neighborhood, and the temptations of his old life. "If I'm going to live a new life," he told me, "I probably need to get out of town."

I talked with the director of the Four Mounds Foundation, the group that helped us take our Near North teams to Iowa. He agreed to hire Sam as a camp counselor and gave him the special assignment of helping to direct activities and to work with the inner-city kids we sent out there to camp, as well as with troubled Iowa kids who needed special help. So after living his entire life on the streets of Chicago (or in jail), Sam Dillon got out of Dodge and moved to Dubuque.

I don't know if all born-again killers would make great camp counselors. But Sam had a way with kids. When he spoke, they listened. And he'd been the one who took Rocket under his wing that week and found out about the abuse.

Darron Kirkman had a very different story.

I met Darron through Dale Craft, a friend of mine from the Fellowship of Christian Athletes who had just taken a coaching job at nearby Collins High School on the West Side. Dale had no financial resources and no booster-club support for his football program. So I got some of my friends to chip in to buy some new helmets and other basic equipment. We also helped finance a weight room. And for a couple of years, Tina and I hosted the Friday-night pregame meals for the entire football team at our house. They had only twenty-five players on the squad, but those guys could eat!

Collins High had an incredible backfield. The halfback, Henry Bailey, went on to set all kinds of school records in college at UNLV and then signed with the Browns in the NFL. Darron Kirkman was his blocking back at Collins, an outstanding 6-foot, 240-pound fullback who scored twenty-six touchdowns himself his senior season.

I was shocked when Darron knocked on my door one day that next fall and said he didn't know what he was going to do. For some reason, no colleges recruited him even though his ACT scores were high enough to make him eligible anywhere. He said he remembered me from those pregame training meals when I'd told him if he ever needed anything to let me know.

I gave him a job working for me, delivering documents, word processing, answering the office phones. I remember asking him one day, "Darron, why do you always go around with your head down? Why don't you look me in the eye when we're talking?"

He said, "Because everyone around here looks like they know what they're doing. And I don't."

I knew that was a breakthrough moment for Darron. I said, "Then fake it till you make it." And I told him that's what I'd done at my first suit and tie job.

Darron also moved in downstairs, and I started making phone calls on his behalf to football coaches around the country. A friend of mine who coached at Pacific Lutheran told me about a junior college coach in California, a Christian guy, who might take him. So the following year, we sent Darron to Foothill Junior College in San Jose, where he started and was a star player on their team until he got so homesick and discouraged that he quit and returned to Chicago before the end of his freshman football season.

I had learned that "got homesick" is often a euphemism for the guilt laid on city kids who are succeeding by those who are not. So the next year, I convinced Darron he needed to go back. But the coach wouldn't let him play that season. Made him pay his dues as equipment manager. Darron grew up and stuck it out. He went back the third fall and broke every running record in school history. Darron got married and had two daughters (in that order) while in college. He played his fourth and fifth years on scholarship for Oregon State, graduated, got named All-Pac 10 fullback, and was leading rusher in the North-South all-star game that's held on Christmas Day every year.

There were several other guys who lived in our basement for various lengths of time during those early years. A client's drug-addicted brother. Guys referred from Prison Fellowship. And one of Dale Craft's assistant coaches at Collins—a white Christian college graduate who'd never had a drink or used drugs in his life. That young man got quite a cross-cultural education living and becoming friends with the likes of Galen and Sam.

Naturally, the attack on Tina had prompted some serious soul-searching about the risk of continuing to live in the city. But it was after all the publicity about Anthony Garrett and the Dantrell Davis shooting in Cabrini-Green that friends and relatives asked if we weren't afraid to live where we did and have a basement apartment housing guys I was trying to help.

"Are you kidding?" I would say. "I'm just waiting to see what happens to the first unfortunate burglar who tries to break into our place. He won't stand a chance against the guys in our basement. The toughest characters in the neighborhood live with us."

EXPANSION

The Muzikowski's basement was soon full.

But 1994 turned out to be such a great year in my business that we actually began looking at vacation homes on the other side of Lake Michigan. We'd spent a few fun weekends over there with friends and their families. It was only an hour or so away—the other side of the lake was to Chicagoans what the Hamptons are to New Yorkers. And I'd sometimes dreamed of owning a vacation home, so it seemed like a reasonable goal.

On the other hand, I kinda knew too much. I realized a getaway home would be a big-ticket possession that we'd use no more than a few weeks and weekends a year. We could let other people use it, of course. But upkeep could become an expensive, time-consuming hassle.

At that same time, my minister was working me over with his sermons. When we'd moved to the West Side, we'd left LaSalle Street Church and its mostly commuter congregation, hoping to find a strong, multiracial church closer to our neighborhood. Though we didn't find one within walking distance, we did find and quickly joined a church in the Humboldt Park neighborhood on Chicago's Northwest Side where the congregation better reflected the makeup of the city—equal parts white, African-American, and Latino. And a few families with Asian heritage. Our pastor at Armitage Baptist Church, Charles Lyons, had lived and ministered on the West Side for more than a quarter-century. He didn't pull any punches when he preached what Jesus had taught. And I was sitting right up front for focus when I heard, "Do not store up your treasures on earth where moth and rust corrupt and thieves break in and steal. Store up your treasures in heaven. For where your treasures are, there will your heart be also."

I also heard, "To whom much is given, much is expected." And that too made me think. We're not talking about a guilt trip here. I was just thinking the issues through, trying to figure out what God wanted me to do with my business profits. And that's when I got a call from Bob Weeden.

I first met Bob soon after Tina and I moved to Chicago. I'd stopped to talk to a homeless guy who'd asked me for money on the street one afternoon.

"How ya doin', man?" I inquired.

"Not too good today," he admitted.

Right then I recognized the difference between Chicago and New York panhandlers. A New York guy would have given me a story about how he was working on his Ph.D. and needed just ten bucks more for tuition.

This Chicago guy came right out and admitted he wasn't doing well. So I bought him a cup of coffee at one of the original Chicago Starbucks on Jackson Street. His name was Brian. He told me he needed a job. So I helped get him cleaned up and found him a job shining shoes at Sam the Shoe Doctor down near the Board of Trade. He did excellent work.

We became friends and I eventually got Brian a better job, shining shoes in the locker room of the East Bank Club. He could

make a hundred dollars a day in tips there and was doing great—
for a month. Then I got a phone call from my friend, the club
comptroller, wanting to know, "Where's Brian? The shoes are
stacked to the ceiling and he's nowhere to be found."

I figured he went out again, so I went looking for him. I remembered him telling me about a guy he called the Colonel who ran a
Pentecostal Christian drug rehab program down on Sixty-third
Street. I went down to the South Side in hopes I'd find that Brian
had checked himself into the program there. That's when I met the
head of Living Light Ministries, the man they called the Colonel—
the Reverend Bob Weeden.

No Brian. But as Bob gave me the grand tour of their building,
showed me their housing for forty men, and told me about the
program, we compared stories and became friends. I was so
impressed by what I'd seen—in Bob Weeden and in his program—
that I became a regular financial supporter of his ministry. Like
many very effective urban ministries, they were long past broke.

And when Brian showed up at my door, hat in hand, a week
later, I sent him down to Living Light to get straightened out.
Which he did.

As time went by and I referred more guys to Bob Weeden for
help, as I spent more time with Bob, observing his example and
learning more of his story, I became even more respectful of the
man and his work. An imposing figure, standing 6' 3" and a solid
190 pounds, Bob was easy to picture as the feared and forceful
gang leader he'd been during his younger days. I was surprised to
learn he was forty-six years old, because he had the energy and the
bearing of a man ten to fifteen years younger.

As a young man, Bob Weeden had dealt heroin in Chicago and
Detroit while also masterminding a number of bank robberies. He
came to Christ through the ministry of Teen Challenge and turned
himself in to authorities. After he earned an early release, he began
preaching throughout the prison system and searching for his
estranged wife, Angie. He finally found her working as a prosti-

tute in New Orleans. After he convinced her that his life had been changed, some of his new friends led her to Christ, and she and Bob soon began a joint ministry of reaching out to alcoholics, drug addicts, and other people living the kind of lives they had now given up.

Bob and Angie lived right there on Sixty-third Street, in the same run-down but meticulously clean storefront building that housed the Living Light office, the rehab center, and the dorm for the men in their program. They didn't take any salary, carried no health insurance, and had no retirement plan. They still don't. For over twenty years now, they have faithfully and sacrificially ministered to the most troubled and destitute people on the South Side of Chicago. And they do it with servants' hearts.

In addition to his street ministry and drug rehabilitation program, Bob pastored a dynamic church that met in a renovated car dealership adjacent to the Living Light offices. I'll never forget the first time I heard the man preach! He and Angie both have an amazing amount of the King James version of the Bible committed to memory.

But the reason Tina and I regularly attended his Sunday evening services for years was not so much to hear Bob's powerful sermons. It was that his church reminded us so much of the Lamb's Church in New York. All sorts of people showed up to worship together every Sunday night. And at 8 P.M. after the service, all two hundred of us sat down together and ate the delicious chicken dinner Angie lovingly prepared.

For the first five years that I had known him, Bob Weeden had dreamed of finding a place outside the city where he could take those men in his rehab program, to get them away from old temptations, channel their energies into physical labor, perhaps teach them a trade, and subject them to a long and intense discipleship training regimen that would provide the foundation for them to go back into their inner-city communities to live consistent, exemplary, and fruitful Christian lives for the rest of their days.

So when Bob called me from southern Illinois in 1994 to say he was sure he had found the place he always believed God had for his ministry, I wasn't surprised. But when he said that he'd made an offer and written an earnest-money check, and that he didn't have enough money in the bank to cover it but that he knew God would provide, I jumped in my car and headed to McLeansboro. He showed me the property in the rolling hills ten miles out of town. And we immediately made all the arrangements for me to purchase the Valley of Peace, which is what Bob wanted to call the farm.

I didn't exactly advertise our plans for the property. I certainly didn't walk into the Hamilton County courthouse and announce that we were opening an alcohol and drug rehabilitation program on the farm for a mostly minority clientele. Since we were miles from any paved road, we hoped to take possession of the property without a lot of notice. And it did take a while for word to get around about the color of most of our farm's residents. Then graffiti started showing up around town: "Niggers stay out!" "The South shall rise again." A cross was burned on our property. Someone killed forty of our goats one night. But no one was hurt, and the harassment died down as the state police began to patrol the roads around our property.

We eventually began selling hogs and operating our own catfish ponds to provide inexpensive food for the men and to try to make enough money to break even. When many of our New York and Chicago friends donated funds to begin building a dorm big enough to house sixty-four men, more graffiti showed up. A nearby Amish community heard about the antagonism and came over to meet with Bob Weeden. They were so impressed by him and his plans that they sent a whole crew of Amish farmers to help raise the roof for a 26,000-square-foot multipurpose building we'd already poured the foundation for.

And some people don't think God has a sense of humor?

You should have seen this bunch of black alcohol and drug addicts from inner-city Chicago working alongside Amish farmers to build a drug rehab dorm out in the sticks of southern Illinois. Sadly, Jethro and Billy Bob were probably sittin' in their pickup, drinkin' beer, and cussin' up a storm just down the road.

Afterward, Mike Julian, one of the African-American guys in the Living Light program, shook his head in amazement and grinned as he told me about the Amish volunteers. "You know, Bob," he said, "those guys work like we play basketball!"

Then he added, "But they did smell kind of funny."

I laughed. But when I told him, "You didn't smell so great yourself when you walked in off the streets and started this program," he had to agree.

Gradually, open opposition dwindled as the local folks got to know Bob Weeden, heard him speak in some of the area churches, and realized he was always willing to go out of his way to be a good neighbor. So we began to take Little League teams to the farm instead of Iowa for their camping experience, to play other teams around that area and to interact with the Valley of Peace Farm guys. Not only do the majority of our kids need more and stronger male role models in their lives, but so many recovering alcoholics and drug addicts have such deep regrets about the families they've lost and the mistakes they've made with their own children that the Living Light–Little League connection soon proved to be a positive and redemptive experience for everyone involved. Men and boys ended up learning from, and ministering to, each other in a wonderful way that made everything we were trying to do in our neighborhood seem somehow beautifully and powerfully interwoven.

Almost as if Someone had planned it that way!

If ever I doubted the way everything we did was divinely connected, I'd only have to think of Duane Bell.

I had just finished speaking at an AA meeting for Northwestern Hospital's in-patient treatment program when this articulate young patient walked up and said, "I know you. You coach my nephew Kenji Conley in Little League. I've seen you out on the field with the kids."

He introduced himself and we talked a while. He'd grown up in the neighborhood and made it out. Went to college. Worked in the computer department of a big downtown bank. White collar job. Good salary. Enough to start buying cocaine for parties. Got in trouble. His company insurance paid for thirty days of in-patient treatment.

I told him, "When you get out, why don't you look me up?"

When he did come to see me, I said, "Why don't you try giving some time back to the neighborhood by umpiring some of our games?"

He did that too. He knew sports. So he was a very competent ump for us. Only trouble . . . he was a no-show from time to time.

I suspected he was using again. Later he confirmed my suspicions, saying he felt so embarrassed about it that when he came home from work, instead of taking the direct route by Carson Field, he would go seven blocks out of the way to North Avenue and back down Sedgwick. Just so he wouldn't have to see us out there coaching his nephew and the other kids from his neighborhood and feel even more guilty.

Then one night at three o'clock in the morning, the phone rang. To my surprise, it was Duane Bell, sounding scared and mumbling something about "owin' money" and "they're gonna kill me."

I had one foot in a shoe to go get him when it hit me. I had a family now. I couldn't go out at three in the morning to save a guy anymore. He hadn't gotten in trouble just then; he'd gotten in trouble a long time ago. Doin' stuff he knew better than to do.

So I told him, "Get a cab over to my house and tell them to kill you over here."

A few days after that, I told Duane, "I'm going to New York. A friend of mine who played football for Penn State, Bob Polito, has just opened the Bowery Transitional Center on Sixth Street. It's a Christian rehab place. I'm gonna be going there. Come to my office; I'll give you a plane ticket and take you to New York with me."

Sure enough, he showed up at my office carrying one ugly lime-green suitcase. His mom came with him to make sure he got on the plane with me. We flew to Newark; I took him to Manhattan and checked him into this brand-new government-and-privately-funded, faith-based program that was years ahead of its time.

Duane Bell's experience reminded me of an old riddle. Three frogs sat on a log. One of them decided to jump off. How many were left? The correct answer is three. The one frog only decided to jump. He never actually did it.

A lot of addicts decide to change. Duane did change. He experienced a real spiritual transformation, turned his life around, and stayed in New York to work on staff at the Bowery Transitional Center. Which meant he was there to help when the next Little League just sort of happened.

When I was back in New York on business, I sometimes spent time with a friend I'd met weight lifting. I'd known Mike Vranos for years before he'd become one of the most successful guys on Wall Street. He had provided my original introduction to his brother Bill, my assistant coach with the Pygmy.

Mike had endured so many of my stories about working with inner-city kids in our Little League that he wanted me to meet a couple of his Ivy League friends who had left the corporate world to start a school in East Harlem. So we all went to work out one evening and then out for dinner. Dropping off one of the guys afterward, we passed an empty lot on 112th Street between

Madison and Park. I instinctively said, "That would sure make a great Little League field."

"Let's have a meeting," one of the men responded. "We know some people who would like to do that."

On my next trip to New York, I met with five or six guys they pulled together. When I told them about our leagues in Chicago, they committed right there to start a baseball program just like we'd done with Near North. And what a group they put together. Carlos Gauthier, a concerned neighborhood dad, was named the first president of the East Harlem Little League. I agreed to serve in an advisory role as commissioner. Tommy Vitiello, a gold trader and another old weight-lifting buddy, became treasurer and a real driving force in the organization. They recruited most of their volunteers from the commodities exchange, many of whom lived on the Upper East Side within twenty blocks or so of the field. It was very much like the situation we'd had with the Near North Little League. For the kids of East Harlem, there were incredible resources available just a few blocks away.

As with our Cabrini league in Chicago, we had an empty, city-owned property we wanted to use. I remember going with B. J., Russ Jeffrey, and some of the other new officers of the league to a meeting downtown with Bill Shea, namesake of Shea Stadium, to try to get some organizational clout behind our plans. The consensus was, "You'll never get official permission unless you get city council members and the state representatives behind it."

We didn't have the time for that. So we just did it. Figuring this was one of those cases in which it would be easier to get forgiveness than permission, we went to work and started transforming the lot into a baseball field. There was already a backstop there. We cleaned up and leveled out the field, adding benches and dugouts. For weeks we requested help from the Parks Department—no response. But at 7 A.M. on opening day, two city trucks showed up, dumped their loads of infield dirt in chest-high piles, and drove away. A PaineWebber broker by the name of John Dolan, B. J., Tommy Vitiello, and I spent the next three hours frantically spreading the dirt around the field with shovels. Just hoping to make the diamond marginally playable for the league's first scheduled game at 10 A.M. that Saturday morning.

We began and ended the East Harlem Little League's first season playing in constant clouds of dust on that soft dirt infield. Except when rain transformed the diamond into one big muddy bog. Twenty teams and nearly three hundred kids (roughly half were Puerto Rican and half were black) played every game of their season on that field.

Everybody made it work. And the coaches, the kids, and their families declared the whole thing a rousing success.

The following spring, the opening day of the East Harlem Little League's second season dawned crisp and clear. I grabbed a taxi in front of the Downtown Athletic Club, my home away from home when on business in New York. The DAC is on the southern end of Manhattan, so the taxi looped around the tip of the island and headed north up the FDR along the harbor and the East River.

I know it's there every day, but to me that drive was beyond spectacular. What a joy to be flying up the east side of Manhattan—the scene of the crime for me, in a way—on my way to the much-improved home of the program we'd started just the year before.

When the cabbie dropped me at the corner of 112th Street and Park, the new field shone so brilliantly I did a doubletake. No piles of dirt today. In fact, the fresh infield sod looked like an astroturf putting green. What a change!

Chris Madalone, a sales rep for Cellular One, had coached the previous season. He never dreamed his simple request for his company's help would result in this $100,000 renovation bringing baseball back in style for hundreds of poor kids in East Harlem. And Cellular One didn't just provide funds. Their employees came out and worked long weekends with the parents and players to create this gorgeously manicured ballfield—a textbook case of a neighborhood and corporate men and women working together.

By eight o'clock, our old Columbia pub DJ had the public address system revved up and ready for the festivities. Joe Gerace cranked up some Springsteen mixed with salsa music—quite an appropriate combination for the morning in that part of town.

By 9 A.M. the Brooklyn Sym-phony had arrived, along with several Christian major leaguers from Baseball Chapel. The Symphony originally played at Ebbett's Field for the Brooklyn Dodgers. This troop of octogenarian entertainers offered a combination of Three Stooges slapstick and a legitimate ragtime band with trombone, trumpet, and snare drum.

The Little League kids enjoyed the up-close and personal interaction with Yankee players Paul O'Neil, Kevin Maas, and Matt Nokes. The rest of us had a ball with the Sym-phony.

B. J. began the official opening ceremonies with a prayer. Then the CEO of Cellular One introduced Mayor Rudy Guliani, and Little League board member and local grade-school principal Iris Denizac knocked our socks off with rousing renditions of the "Star-Spangled Banner" and "Borinquen," the Puerto Rican anthem. Rudy threw a strike, and the ballplayers ran a clinic for an hour and shared about some of their struggles and their faith with the players, their parents, and fans alike. The local chapter of the ACLU failed to show up to protest the proselytizin'—perhaps because it was early Saturday morning, because this was 112th Street, which needed all the prayer it could get, and because the parents would have run them out of the neighborhood.

I will never forget what happened during the opener, as long I live.

East Harlem is always a loud place when the weather breaks. The sound of sirens, taxi horns, pre-Memorial Day firecrackers, and of course, since the neighborhood was predominantly Puerto Rican, loud Latin rhythms bombarded us from several directions at once.

The crowd remained even after the Yankees, the Sym-phony, and Mayor Guliani all departed. In Chicago we practically begged family members to come out and support their kids; I'd coached some boys for three years and never met another member of the family. In East Harlem, a lot of Puerto Rican dads came out to help coach. And on a Saturday morning, here were parents and grandparents lined three deep along the chain-link fence on 112th Street awaiting the start of the kids' first game.

I came dressed to umpire the opening game behind the plate. Then I planned to catch an afternoon flight back home to Chicago.

Usually our Little League umps in Chicago got quite a work-out calling a whole game alone. But for today's inaugural in New York, we had umps at all four corners of the diamond. We even had an experienced crew—all four recovering alcoholics and addicts. In fact, the umpiring crews for the East Harlem League's entire season were drawn from the Bowery Transitional Center.

This umpire arrangement was a brainstorm that new Bowery Center staffer Duane Bell and I cooked up and prayed about for all of ten seconds before we implemented it. Our idea was to pro-vide men in the program a chance to give back their time. We saw it as a win-win situation: the men got an opportunity for mean-ingful service and the league got a steady supply of umpires.

Daryll R. umped third base. Brand new to the Bowery Tran-sitional Center and still sweating, he was dead serious about the game. Duane covered second base. And Shakur M. rounded out the umpiring crew at first.

Shakur told me he'd become hooked on umpiring for kids on opening day the year before. He said he had been only about five months clean at the time and "got tricked" into coming by Duane. "Before that first game," Shakur said, "I kept hearing this squeaky little voice saying 'Mister, mister.' I ignored it because ... ya know ... I'd been a drug addict for mosta m' life ... and well ... nobody had ever addressed me like that. Then I felt a tug on my arm. It was a little Puerto Rican boy in a baseball uniform, 'round 'bout nine years old.

" 'Mister, can you hold my chain and cross? I'm pitching and the rules say I can't wear them in the game.' "

Shakur said, "I finally realized the kid was talkin' ta me. 'Mister'? Me? Yeah ... if I was a 'mister' out there on that field, I mean, things were lookin' up already."

The Kidder Peabody Reds played the New England Mutual Red Sox in a nine-to-ten-year-old-boys game in our second season opener. The game was well played that morning. Coaches and fans really got into the game.

But about the fifth inning, I kept hearing this loud *wooka, wooka* sound I thought was coming from behind me and across the street. The Red Sox pitcher was warming up when I heard it again, looked up, and spotted the culprit. About ten stories above us in the building behind the backstop, there was a guy leaning out a window with a gun. *Wooka, wooka!* He was shooting at a building across the street from center field.

I quickly gathered my umpiring crew behind the mound and pointed the guy out without actually pointing. A calm debate began there on the mound among my colleagues.

"Guy's shootin' an Uzi," Shakur observed.

"That's no Uzi. It's a Browning nine millimeter," said Daryll.

"No way that's a Browning nine, man," our first base umpire argued.

"You're both wrong," Duane said. "That's a Glock if I ever heard one."

I couldn't believe my ears. We were arguing about the make and caliber of a weapon being fired high above a field where we had a Little League game in progress. I felt like screaming, "This is insanity!" But I didn't want to cause a panic.

"Okay, let's get somebody from Cellular One to call 911 on that guy up there," I said calmly. That decided, I headed back to my position behind home plate.

"Batter up," I called. And our game went on.

Maybe five minutes later, the Boys in Blue arrived and rushed into the building behind us. The shooting stopped. And we finished the game without any further overhead distractions.

Old Coach Gallagher back in Bayonne would have been so proud. We never missed a pitch.

WEST SIDE STORY

Don't drink, don't drug, don't cheat on your wife." I've heard this mantra a thousand times at AA meetings. When I got married, one of my main goals in life was to be the Cal Ripken of one woman. There was no television in our room. When I wasn't working or coaching, I tried to be home with Tina and our growing family.

Living where we did actually made that easier. When I wasn't running to work, my commute downtown was just a four-minute cab ride, a huge plus I thought outweighed any negatives of our neighborhood. I prized any extra hours I could squeeze out of a day because parenthood had quickly proven to Tina and me that quality time happens during quantity time. And by early 1995, we needed all the time we could get with four kids and a fifth on the way.

Here's a look at our roster that year.

Six-year-old Sammie was a real fish in the swimming pool but showed little interest in baseball; already her favorite sports were singing and swimming. It was too early to tell about any athletic interests her younger sister might have, but toddler Tanner was already demonstrating both the speed and the determination to keep up with her older siblings.

Four-year-old Bo was a pure lefty. He viewed his brother, Isaiah, who was just fourteen months younger, as his personal Kewpie doll. Bo would routinely stick a baseball glove on his little brother's hand and begin firing away. The scary thing was, Ikey liked it.

These were the same two boys who helped our family make a lasting impression at the suburban country club of one of my friends later that year. It was one of those unforgettable parenting moments you see happening in slow motion but are unable to prevent.

Bo had climbed the high dive and was now contemplating the wisdom of that decision and the reality of his lofty predicament as he stood at the end of the board. I watched from my seat by the ladder, waiting to welcome the doggie-paddler after the jump.

Next in line on the ladder, Ike grew impatient with the delay. So he strutted out onto the board and attempted to kick his brother off. A wrestling match ensued. The attention of everyone around the club's pool was suddenly riveted on the drama developing overhead. There was a collective gasp and perhaps a stifled scream or two as the grapplers plunged off the board and continued contesting their courage until the surface of the water smacked them apart.

I fished my semistunned sons out of that pool with the assistance of so many lifeguards, supervisors, and alarmed club members that you'd have thought no one had ever before witnessed such behavior from two small boys. *There goes the neighborhood, right?* I tried not to laugh when three-year-old Ike told me it was "just like Robin Hood and Little John."

So where on the West Side were Robin Hood and Little John, and hopefully their fair sisters, going to play baseball when their time came? You had to be nine before you could play in the Near North Little League program, and our 1991 move to the West Side had taken us outside the boundaries of that league. The Englewood league ended the year before. East Harlem was in New York. And there was no way we were going to commute to one of the "nice parks" in some "better" neighborhood so my children could play in an all-white league that charged each player 85- to 125-dollar registration fees and uniform costs and thereby priced out any poor kids "unintentionally."

I didn't see that we had any other choice. If our new neighborhood was going to have a youth baseball league our kids could play in someday, someone was going to have to start it. Tina and I looked at each other and thought, *Here we go again.*

I guess we could have waited a couple of years until our kids were old enough to play. But there were other peoples' children in the neighborhood who were ready to play now. And a number of West Side kids, some of whom had followed us there from the Cabrini neighborhood, were already traveling across town to play in the Near North league because there wasn't a comparable free program any closer.

The projects on the West Side of Chicago were every bit as volatile as Cabrini-Green, but without the hype. Cabrini's proximity to trendy Lincoln Park and its downtown location attracted journalists like candy attracts kids. The press treated Cabrini like a drunken uncle they let live in the back room. The uncle provided them with ready material they could report but not remedy.

On the West Side, when kids got killed, it didn't even make the paper. The gunfire coming out of Rockwell Gardens, the ABLA Homes, Henry Horner Homes, and the nearby neighborhood lowrises was as ominous as anything we had experienced around Cabrini.

In addition to those large and decaying housing projects, the West Side was home to Cook County Hospital (the inspiration behind the popular TV show *ER*), the veterans administration, and several homeless shelters.

The Good Samaritan in Jesus' parable could've easily found full-time work on our block.

The front doorbell would ring.

"Need money for food."

"Here is food."

"No, I need *money* 'for food,' not just food."

Or, "Need money for diapers for my baby."

"Okay, here are diapers."

"No, I need *money* for diapers" *(hiccup)*.

In our alley, men with shopping carts collected cans and any metal they could find. One Saturday, I observed through my back window a man ripping a twenty-foot drainpipe right off the house behind us. I thought my neighbor, Dean, a retired Cubs grounds-keeper, must be losing his mind in the hundred-degree summer heat, but it wasn't Dean. The man stomped and folded my neighbor's drainpipe until it would fit into his shopping cart with the cans. I ran down to confront the perpetrator, who tried to flee pushing his tin-laden cart. When I cornered him, I realized he had Down's syndrome and was frightened to death. Shoot, Dean needed a new drainpipe anyway. So Dean, our new friend the Tin Man, and I had lunch and purchased the new pipe. It took a couple of hours, but Dean and I laughed till we cried in the process.

Scouting around, I found three locations in our neighorhood where I thought Little League baseball could be played. Just down the street from where we lived was a vacant, rock- and litter-strewn city block owned by a state agency—the Illinois Medical District. That meant it belonged to all the citizens of the state and was subject to input from our elected and appointed officials. It wouldn't have to be an us-versus-them thing. The field already belonged to all of us. At least that's how we chose to look at it as we jumped the fence and walked around trying to decide what needed to be done before we could play games there.

The second location, Touhy Herbert Field, three blocks west of the United Center, already had a small softball diamond with a dirt infield and a very nice adjacent playground. Chicago Bulls owner Jerry Reinsdorf had provided the park for area children when half the neighborhood was paved over to make a parking lot at the new stadium he built as a home for the Bulls, the Blackhawks, and major concerts. The James Jordan Boys and Girls Club (named after Michael's father) was under construction beyond right field. But no league currently used the diamond, and frankly, it was a rough spot.

The third location was Altgeld Park, ten blocks west of our home. It boasted three full diamonds in playable condition. I pounded on the locked doors of the Altgeld field house until a Parks District employee who managed the facility finally peeked out the door, determined I was no threat to her, and let me in. She confirmed what I'd already determined—no organized teams used any of the fields at that time.

I'd learned a thing or two starting the first three Little Leagues. I now knew there are dedicated teachers in every neighborhood who can provide a wealth of contacts, serve as excellent resources themselves, and become valuable allies. So I called on a couple of guys I'd met at local schools and asked them to help me implement a very scientific strategy I'd developed to determine which of the three locations would attract the necessary sampling of children to project a successful baseball league.

I gave them each a full equipment bag, twelve baseballs, and strict instructions. "Take this bag to the field. Start playing catch—with yourself, or better yet, with a friend. See if any kids come out to play with you. Okay, let's have a prayer together and get going."

That was it. Mike Clark, a teacher at St. Callistus Catholic School a couple of blocks from my house, took the empty medical district lot. Mike, who was a tremendous athlete himself, had two batboy-age sons of his own. By the end of the week, he had a hundred kids out there following him around.

Mike was joined by local public-school teacher Charlie Gunn. Soon there were two hundred kids at the field that wasn't even a field yet.

I took my equipment bag to Touhy Herbert Field. The scene there was better—or worse, depending on your perspective. Kids swarmed like bees to honey, many of them from the Henry Horner homes just across the street from the United Center. A few years earlier, a *Wall Street Journal* urban affairs reporter wrote a book about these projects. *There Are No Children Here* won numerous awards and accolades. Reviewers called it "gripping," "heart-wrenching," and "stirring." But was anything ever done in response? Who was going to pick the kids up and take them to practice tomorrow?

Over a hundred kids came out and it was only Monday.

When I talked to them about wanting to start a league, a couple of the boys ran "to get Mandeldove." I had no idea what they meant until they returned with Andre Mandeldove in tow—all 6′ 5″, 275 pounds of him. He introduced himself as a teacher at St. Malachy's over on Oakley. He already had enough boys for a team in each age level. But he had no equipment and no one to play.

So I told him about our plans for the league, quickly explaining how it would be like the programs at Near North and East Harlem. "Oh, man!" Andre exclaimed with a grin. "I've been praying for something like this for a long time!"

The next day, I took my bag of equipment and headed to Altgeld Park with my friend Leo Wisniewski, former noseguard for the Indianapolis Colts, whose brother was all-pro for the Oakland Raiders. Leo had recently moved to the West Side to work with a charitable organization called Athletes and Business for Kids. There at Atgeld, the kids again crowded around us; some of them thought Leo was Arnold Schwarzenegger.

Our "scientific study" told us all we needed to know. Everywhere we went, the neighborhood was overflowing with kids who wanted to play baseball. So Andre, Mike, Charlie, Tina, and I formed a board to officially become the Near West Little League.

We used much the same strategy I'd used five years before in the Cabrini neighborhood. I went to friends who had resources and asked them to match me and help sponsor and coach a team in our new league.

In many ways, that was a little easier this time around. The idea didn't seem so radical since we now had a track record we could point to. And we even had people living in our new neighborhood who had seen and been part of the Near North league's success—players and their families, as well as supporters and coaches who were eager to see the same thing happen with Near West.

My old college friend, Joe Guinan, was now president of Fuji Futures. He'd been a big reason we had moved into the SoNo neighborhood near Cabrini when we first came to Chicago. And after Tina and I moved to the West Side, Joe bought a double lot and built a home just a block away. He would be a major supporter of the new league just as he'd been with Near North.

The three existing diamonds at Altgeld Park were more than we'd had when we started the Cabrini league. But there were so many kids in the neighborhood, we felt certain we would need more. That's why we decided that forgiveness would be easier to get than permission and jumped the fence again at the Illinois Medical District property to begin transforming that empty lot into a baseball field. In the month we had before opening day, we dug out the rocks and hauled away the trash. We marked off the field with both sixty- and ninety-foot base paths and erected a backstop and two dugouts. We purchased and laid the sod with the help of a crew of volunteers from suburban Willow Creek Church and my own personal street gang (actually, Bob Weeden and ten hardworking men from Living Light).

One day while we were out working on the new field, a car stopped, and a man in a suit and tie got out and walked over to ask what we were doing. So I told him. It turned out the man's name was David Livingston, the governor's executive director of the Illinois Medical District, whose "abandoned" property we had so brazenly appropriated and had almost finished transforming into a beautifully landscaped Little League field. I don't know what amazed David most, our good intentions, what we'd already done with the property, or our gall. But he was so impressed that he arranged to have papers drawn up and signed to make it official: the Illinois Medical District would lease the property to the Near West Little League to be used as a baseball field—for the price of one dollar a year.

We didn't sign anything official with the Parks District to use the three diamonds at Altgeld. We just told them we were coming after we announced the formation of the league and sent flyers to all the local schools.

Mayor Daley accepted our invitation to throw the ceremonial first pitch during opening day festivities. He was so overwhelmed by the turnout—both the number of kids in uniforms and the family members there for our big community cookout—that he pulled me aside to say he thought what we were doing was great. "What else do you guys need?" he wanted to know. "If there is anything I can do to help, give me a call."

At times, the local press could go pretty hard on the mayor, but I saw that the man had a passion for the children of Chicago that was intense and real. I hoped he saw that we shared that same intensity. I mean, he had to have been impressed with our new field. And he would have been even more impressed if he'd come by at midnight the night before and seen some of our volunteers plus a crew of Living Light guys finish surfacing the infield, which we had illuminated with the headlights of the cars we parked strategically around the field.

We fielded twenty-eight teams our inaugural season—the summer of 1995. Not only was Near West the largest first-year program we'd ever started, it served a broader range of children. While the new league was predominantly African-American, about 20 percent was Latino, along with a handful of white kids. We offered everything from T-ball for our smallest players to baseball with official ninety-foot base paths for our teenage teams. And this time we also had girls' divisions for Little League softball.

Experience had convinced me of the importance of offering girls' programs, because so many of the girls I'd met over the years living and coaching baseball in the city reminded me of anything but an urban image. They were like deer caught in the headlights. Frozen by fear and uncertainty. Often abused by adult men. And incredibly vulnerable underneath a tough exterior.

Anyone who thinks so many little adolescent girls of eleven and twelve and thirteen are getting pregnant by their middle-school boyfriends needs to do more research. The real shame is this travesty has been repeated generation after generation.

One evening while umpiring at Altgeld Park, I met a woman who looked about my age sitting in the stands at one of our games. When I introduced myself and asked if she was there to watch her son play, she laughed and pointed out her twelve-year-old grandson.

In an attempt to ease any awkwardness and compliment her at the same time, I assured her that she didn't look old enough to be anyone's grandmother. She proudly told me she was forty-two and that she was in fact a great-grandmother, since her grandson's sister had just had her first baby.

You do the math!

STEALIN' HOME

We had determined from the beginning that there would be another difference in the Near West league. We would make it crystal clear to everyone at the outset that this was a faith-based program. We unapologetically employed a Christian focus.

If anyone had a problem with that, we figured we'd refer them to the official Little League pledge printed in the official Little League rule book: "I trust in God, I love my country and will respect its laws. I will play fair and strive to win. But win or lose, I will always do my best."

A bit old-fashioned, perhaps. But versus what? 2 Live Crew rap music? Ya ever hear the words to some of those songs?

I mean when the sun's comin' up over the Sears Tower on a Saturday morning in May, it shines on kids and families of all different colors gathered to play this great game. Picture Marcus Nance, an ex-Marine from our church who is now in med school, with his hand on his heart singing the national anthem. There is electricity in the air, and the grills are on for all you can eat. Life is good in our Near West neighborhood. So it seems ludicrous to give in to the God-is-dead theory on opening day.

Most of our players are from single- or no-parent households and attend public schools in which scheduled prayer is banned. But most of our coaches and kids—black, white, and Hispanic—are members of churches. Among those who are not, some of our best coaches, including one of my closest friends in the league, Ken Alpart, are Jewish. So Ken stepped to the microphone and read from the Proverbs of Solomon on opening day.

We refused to pretend there is no God because five out of five hundred people might feel uncomfortable. The bottom line is I never, ever, had a parent complain that we began all our meetings, programs, and games with prayer.

In fact, the opposite is true. They soon expected and encouraged it. Because almost everyone who knew anything about our league understood it was faith that motivated the start of the league and that it was our faith that kept us coming back.

The Near West Little League even encouraged church-sponsored teams. And the half dozen West Side churches were a real benefit to the organization. How refreshing it was to have so many teams you could count on to show up on schedule and play their games without arguing among themselves or hassling the umpires.

Not that everything went without a hitch. But we'd expected there would be challenges—in part because our fields were so accessible and heavily utilized.

On hot summer days, we hooked hoses to nearby fire hydrants to enable our volunteers and our players to water down the infields and cool each other off at the same time. And we eventually learned how to play and win a most irritating game we called "stealing home."

I played this game for years in the Cabrini Little League. I'd grown so weary of it that I gladly handed the assignment over to our first Near West Little League summer intern, J. R. Gardner. After depending entirely on volunteer labor for years in the various leagues we'd started, we had finally decided to seek summer work relief by starting a college intern program. J. R., a twenty-one-year-old shortstop from Geneva College (a Christian school in Pennsylvania), was our first recruit. His job was to help coach, fill in as umpire, drive the vans to pick up and drop off kids, take players to camps, and maintain the fields. Including home plate.

I understood the challenge far better than J. R. did. So in my detailed orientation instructions, I told him, "I hate to tell you this, J. R. But you need to understand. Anything not nailed down disappears from our ballfields. Anything! You got that?"

"Yes, sir!" he replied.

"So you have to pull up all the bases on every diamond at the end of the last game each night."

"Yes, sir."

"And you can't let anyone steal home plate."

"Home plate?" I could almost see his mind working as he processed this information. Like he couldn't quite believe it or wondered if I was serious.

"Yep," I told him. "The plates are thick, heavy rubber that cost us about forty bucks apiece. So if you don't want to reset every diamond six days a week, you gotta figure out a way to keep 'em from stealin' home. Okay?"

"Okay," he nodded determinedly.

A serious baseball guy and a real stickler for details, J. R. wielded a professional builder's tape to carefully align our five diamonds—all meticulously measured off of five new home plates, each of which were firmly imbedded six inches deep in the ground.

I have no idea how to calculate the street value of an only slightly used home plate. But someone was evidently about to find out. Because the second day of our season, J. R. was already 0 for 5. When he arrived to line the fields for that evening's games, all five home plates had vanished. With empty holes left in their places.

With the help of his father, who had just arrived from Pennsylvania for a visit, J. R. determined to put an end to this "game" once and for all. Armed with two-by-fours, hammers, nails, large tin cans, cement, and water buckets, this father-son duo reminded me of Bill Murray versus the golf-course ground-hogs in *Caddy Shack*.

The Gardners dug halfway to China and gave our home plates such deep, deep roots that we never lost another one. They were all still there when J. R. came back for a recent visit with his wife and three volunteer students to help paint fences and lay fresh sod on our fields. (Give me a hundred committed young men like J. R. and we could transform the entire West Side.)

Despite the annoyances of petty vandalism, things went incredibly well for the Near West league that first year. In fact, we figured the league's projected expansion the following summer would mean there would be no way to schedule all of our second season games—even if we used Altgeld's three diamonds, the Illinois Medical District field, and Touhy Herbert Field. We desperately needed lights so we could play more games after dark.

Mayor Daley had said to let him know if there was anything we needed. It was time to see if we could take him at his word.

The answer was yes. We wrote a Near West Little League check to the Chicago Parks District for the downstroke, and Mayor Daley and the city paid the rest. As a result, we opened the following season with Altgeld's three diamonds lit up like Comiskey Park. The Near West Little League was now taking back the night.

Chicago Parks District Superintendent Forrest Claypool almost took out a nearby photographer with his ceremonial pitch. And we held one brightly lit barbecue for five hundred people from our neighborhood. It was thrilling to see hundreds of fans gathered to watch four excited teams warming up under the new lights.

Our league's first two night games were about to begin. So of course, I was short one plate umpire.

The city electrician and some people from Sylvania lighting wanted to meet right after the lights went on. There was no way

I could fill in and ump the opener. I needed to draft a volunteer, and fast.

I jogged over to the backstop where I'd left some brand-new umpire gear, still wrapped in plastic, behind home plate. I picked up the shin guards, clicker, mask, and chest protector, dropping the plastic-wrapped mask as I stepped off the field and out of the bright lights. But as I reached down for the mask, a huge weather-beaten hand beat me to it.

I stood up slowly to find myself facing an extremely large man who had begun taking the mask out of the plastic like a child unwrapping a Christmas present.

"G-game tonight? G-gonna play tonight?" he asked.

"Yes, sir," I replied. "I need an umpire, though; can't start without one. So if you'll just give me that mask, I'll . . ."

"C-cubs won today," he said. "Yup, beat the Cardinals 4-1. I t-tape all the games."

"Great," I responded, thinking, *Didn't the Cubs play the Cincinnati Reds today?* But I was scanning the sidelines now, looking for someone whose arm I could twist to get my *volunteer* umpire.

"Hey, I gotta go," I said, reaching for the mask the big man was holding. It didn't budge. We were both holding it now.

"I-I-I can umpire. I b-been knowin' baseball all my life."

At that point, I heard someone calling my name. Seemed I was needed "right now" at the field house so the experts could explain the timing devices for the new lights.

So I gave up and let go of the mask. The giant put it on, bent down on one knee, and started buckling on a shin guard.

Clearly, there would be no stopping him. "Here's your clicker," I said, handing him the plastic ball-strike-out counter. I had no idea whether he understood how to use it or even knew what it was. *I'll have to come right back to check on him. But I gotta go now.*

The giant stood up and crushed me with a bear hug.

"Can I k-keep these? I c-can keep 'em, right?"

"Sure, man." The guy seemed so determined to have them. And he was a big guy. "Good luck." We shook hands and smiled together. His smile revealed fewer, but much larger, teeth than mine.

I shoulda known. What was supposed to be a five-minute assignment in the field house with the lighting experts turned into a one-hour seminar. I didn't get back out on the fields until the fourth inning. *Shoot. I forgot all about that first-time umpire. I better check on him.* I began to trot past the packed basketball courts, heading to the fields. I was a hundred yards away when I heard a booming voice. "Steee-rike three!" The call came from the giant.

Amazing! This big, shy, soft-spoken man who mumbled to himself and stammered and struggled just to converse had become a take-charge umpire who administered a baseball game with utmost confidence. I had only to stand by and watch in wonder the remainder of that game as he barked out balls and strikes with authority and made sure all batters' shirts were tucked in—with no sideways hats permitted. He even once correctly called the infield-fly rule, an obscure regulation so seldom used that a lot of our coaches probably didn't understand it. He'd obviously been telling the truth when he claimed, "I been knowin' baseball all my life."

After the game, I shared a burger with my new best friend. He told me his name was Miles Blackman. I didn't know it then, but Miles and I would eat together often over the coming years as he became a regular dinner companion and frequent guest in the Muzikowski household.

Miles may have been a guy who had trouble getting organized and managing life outside the lines. But he had the baseball rule book memorized. "It was a g-good game," he told me that first night. "But I had to eject that one c-coach for coming out of the box too much. Hey, d-did ya hear the Cubs beat the Pirates today?"

That's funny. I really was sure they'd played the Reds.

The very next morning, I received a 7 A.M. phone call from a Parks District maintenance man. "You better come down here, Coach." So I did. The guy, who was on the verge of tears he was so angry, showed me what had happened during the night. Vandals had pried open a metal panel at the base of each new light tower, reached inside, and yanked all the copper wire down from where it had been attached at the top, gutting every single light pole. They may have gotten fifty dollars' worth of copper wire per pole. What we got was aggravation and frustration over a baseball schedule that had to be revised and revised again for a month before we could get all the lights rewired.

This time the maintenance crew ignored code and welded each pole's panels shut. Forget the timing system that was programmed to come on whenever we played. The lights now turned on every night at dusk and stayed on till dawn, which reduced vandalism and a lot of other illicit activity that used to take place in and around Altgeld Park.

The kids in the league were so angry about the month of cancelled night games, they told me they hoped the next person who tried to mess with the lights got electrocuted. Then we could bury him under one of the pitcher's mounds.

It could get a little crazy at Altgeld Park on a Friday night. Especially once our lights could be seen and attracted people from miles away. The good news was we were right on the Eisenhower

Expressway where there's easy access off and on. The bad news was . . . we were right on the Eisenhower. And if you were driving by shooting a gun, you didn't have to slow down.

I saw it happen only once, but once was enough. A car came speeding along the service road which parallels two of our Little League baselines.

Dukadukadukaduka.

Kids and fans were diving all over. People screamed. The homeless guys sat frozen on the benches. It was over as soon as it started. Ten seconds. Nobody hurt. Sirens on the way.

Play ball!

We did have some fallout after the drive-by. The day after the shooting, I received a long recorded message on my answering machine from a suburban church's volunteers. The recording went something like this: "Bob, this is Buff and Biff. We are not going to be available to coach anymore. We still support your vision for the league. And we still have a heart for inner-city kids. But we had only seven boys show up for practice the other day. Our record is 2-7. And we sincerely feel we're not called to coach. We feel God has closed the door to this ministry for us. But we will continue to pray for you."

Just great! I thought. *Lord, save me from your followers!* But I didn't bother to return the call or pursue the resigning coaching staff. I'd had enough experience with some evangelical churches over the past ten years to interpret their early retirement speech, which they had so carefully phrased in what I call "Christianese"— a language popular with people who want to sound spiritual and even misuse Scripture in order to gloss over or justify their own behavior.

"Still support your vision" really means "It's getting a little hairy out there. I'm sick of these kids, and it takes too much time. Good luck."

"Have a heart for inner-city kids" means "I feel sad for a minute when I see a dead kid's picture in the paper."

"Not called to do it" means "I miss my Saturday golf game—which I can't say I'm called to either. But I need the quiet time. After all, Jesus took quiet time. See you at the men's retreat." *Sorry boys! You can't retreat unless you first attack.*

"God closed the door" often means "It got hard, so I quit." You can be sure God wouldn't have closed the door on my quitting coaches if their team's record had been 9-0.

We'll "pray for you" usually doesn't mean anything. If everyone who promised to pray for me really did, I'd be levitating. It happens so often that when I have other Christians tell me "I'll pray for you," I'm tempted to say, "Don't pray for me. Either coach third base or umpire the two o'clock game next Saturday afternoon."

It's not that I don't value people's prayers. I do. But any little old lady in a nursing home who can't get out of bed can pray. And a lot of them do. What we need even more are volunteers we can count on. To show up on time. And not quit halfway through the season.

J. R. and I took over that coachless team, even though we were each coaching two other teams already. When ten players showed up for our game that next night, our young intern and I were all over the sidelines offering encouragement and cheers, "Yeah, baby; yeah, baby; yeah!" Although I really wanted to win that one, we got beat in a close one. But we were there and we were in the game.

We stayed in the game even after another incident of random, insane firepower.

There is almost no such thing as self-service at certain West Side gas stations. The homeless guys insist on pumpin' it for you at Roosevelt and Western Avenue for a buck. But from me, they always get ice-cold juice and a Living Light Valley of Peace invitation.

I was standing next to this homeless guy sharing my sobriety one beautiful summer evening. I had already paid for the gas and delivered candy to my two oldest sons, Bo and Ike. They were sharing the bag of Skittles in the seat of the Little League van with the sliding door open for ventilation while we were stopped to fill up.

One of the boys dropped the candy bag, and Skittles scattered all over the van floor. Some rolled out the door onto the ground. The boys scrambled to salvage their treats when *bam!* Glass shattered all around the tiny bullet hole in the van's side window. Yet the fragmented window remained in place.

I instinctively looked into the van for my boys. They weren't there! But even as my heart sank, two little heads popped back up into sight from their candy hunt.

"Wow! What happened?" Ike asked.

"Dad, who broke the window?" Bo wanted to know.

"I'm getting outta here," exclaimed the homeless guy.

As he took off, I looked up and down the streets. Nothing. No one ran. No tires screeched. The shot had come out of nowhere, maybe blocks away.

I turned back and looked at my boys. Saved by the spilled Skittles.

In our unpredictable world, none of us can protect ourselves or our families from every danger, no matter how hard we try. When God is going to take you, he's going to take you. So we have a choice. We can sit on the sidelines in a constant state of worry and fear. Or we can get in the game and trust God to help us deal with whatever happens—not only to us but to our children, Sammie, Bo, Ike, Tanner, Luke (born in 1995), and Scout (born in 1997 and named for the little girl in my favorite novel, Harper Lee's *To Kill a Mockingbird*).

During our league's second or third season, the Chicago Police Department made one of the biggest drug busts in Chicago street-gang history right in the Altgeld field house. A local Vice Lords leader named Bebe, whom I'd met playing hoops there at the park, was busted along with several of his lieutenants by undercover cops who had infiltrated the gang, confiscated kilos of evidence, and sent the culprits to prison.

The Near West Little League continued to play ball, growing every summer until we became the largest inner-city Little League baseball program in America. Last year over six hundred kids played on forty-eight teams in seven divisions. Not only are our fields lighted now, but we recently installed an underground watering system that we hope will keep the grass on our diamonds so lush that we'll make the Cubs' and White Sox' grounds crews green with envy.

We had no delusions about saving the world. We might not be able to change the fact that some kids living in our Near West neighborhood have to do without. But we can see that they play baseball every summer on fields that are second to none.

In 1998, when we learned our good friend and supporter David Livingston, the Illinois Medical District's executive director, was dying with cancer, we held a moving ceremony in which we officially named the medical district diamond Livingston Park, in honor of our benefactor's lasting commitment to children of the Near West community. David wasn't the only one who cried that day.

We purchased bronze statues titled *Siblings*—of a young boy in a baseball uniform with his sister—to place at the newly landscaped entrance to Livingston Park. One of my Old Blue rugby pals, Tom Sloan, loaded the statues on the back of his pickup truck and drove straight through from Colorado to get them to Chicago in time for the ceremony. My friend and engineer extraordinaire Bill Lavicka and I cemented steel posts inside the spines of the hollow metal figures and then anchored the statues in a concrete base.

Those precautions soon proved necessary. Within a week after we dedicated the field and the sculptures, someone tied a chain around our statues and tried in vain to yank them out. When I saw the tire marks on the sidewalk the next morning, I laughed and hoped they tore the rear end off their car. We installed lights to illuminate the statues at night and to discourage further vandalism. It worked. If you drive by Livingston Field today, you can still see the bronze statues of a Little League girl and boy—holding an only slightly bent baseball bat. The sign underneath says, "Livingston Park. Home of the Near West Little League."

Miles Blackman became another familiar fixture of the NWLL. After opening night in 1996, he kept showing up, every day of that season and every one since. Five or six days a week, Miles umpires our games. He's been honored as the league's volunteer of the year so many times we've joked that all we have to do for our annual awards banquet is change the date on Miles' plaque.

He's a threatening figure with a gentle soul who can easily be misunderstood. I remember getting a Thanksgiving-morning phone call from the Chicago PD's precinct over on Monroe. It was Miles. He had been arrested and he didn't understand why. I rushed over to the precinct to sort things out.

I learned Miles had been walking down a neighborhood street when he noticed construction going on in an old row house just a few streets away from where we lived. Curious to see what was going on inside and wanting to be friendly to any newcomers to our neighborhood, Miles had walked in through an open door and absolutely terrified a yuppie couple who were remodeling the place and looked up suddenly to see this hulk of a black man standing inside their door. Before they realized he had just wanted to say hello, they called 911, and the cops roared up and were forced to charge Miles with criminal trespassing.

Fortunately, the cops at the precinct knew Miles and they knew me. So they refused my bail offer and let me take him home for Thanksgiving with our family. The charges were dropped the next week.

A funnier incident with Miles took place a while back when Dan Quayle was contemplating a run for the Republican presidential nomination. He must have known about our league because of the Points of Light Award we received from the first Bush administration. And I guess he was trying to stir up some urban support for his candidacy. His advance people contacted us through a friend to say that while he was scheduled to be in Chicago to attend a downtown Republican fund-raiser, Quayle would like to stop by for a quick visit during one of our Little League night games at Altgeld Park. We didn't know exactly what to expect, but we warned players, coaches, and fans ahead of time that the former vice president would be coming and that we needed to be on our best behavior.

The appointed evening arrived, and so did Dan Quayle and his entourage. We quickly ushered them into the field house for a quick introduction to various league and neighborhood officials. Everyone stood in a circle and held hands as Bob Weeden led a brief prayer. Then we headed out to the field where the former VP would throw out a ceremonial first pitch and say a few words to our players and fans.

As we exited through the field house door and started down the narrow sidewalk, there was Miles hurrying toward us, dripping with sweat from calling one game already, and now blocking our way down the sidewalk. He looked up, startled, saw me, and immediately recognized the guests he'd obviously forgotten were coming.

He gave us all a huge gap-toothed grin and exclaimed, "Dan Quayle, my man! How's it goin' you ..." and he cordially addressed Vice President Quayle in street terms the crude likes of which obviously startled the politician. But to his credit, Quayle realized Miles' friendly intent with the vulgarity and reached out to shake the big man's meaty hand. I had a difficult time not bursting into laughter as Miles seized Quayle's hand, drew him close, threw a big sweaty arm over the shoulder of the politician's freshly pressed golf shirt, and said, "Come have your 'pitcher' taken with me, Quayle."

You gotta love this. I can still visualize that scene—a relatively diminutive Dan Quayle grinning gamely while he stood helplessly clamped in the grasp of our league's most faithful volunteer as cameras flashed.

Not all of my most vivid league-related memories took place on our Near West fields. Or even in our neighborhood.

Sadly, despite the quality of our facilities and all the years we've run our leagues without any serious on-the-field casualties, we still have trouble finding teams from other Little Leagues who are willing to play us at home on the Near West Side. On the bright side, this has meant we've been able to have some great experiences taking road trips to play outside of the city. A lot of our teams drive to the suburbs to play exhibition games every year. We still take kids to visit the Living Light Farm and play downstate teams. And for a few years now, we've had a special arrangement with a Christian camp down in the Ozarks called Kids Across America so that all the boys and girls on teams in our league have the option of a weeklong camp experience each summer.

But one of the most memorable trips I've ever been on was the year my twelve-year-olds all-star team was invited to the first annual Knoxville Shootout, a big invitational tournament over the Fourth of July weekend. As usual, we had players who'd never been out of Chicago, let alone seen the Great Smoky Mountains of Tennessee.

We made a week of it, playing one game in downstate Illinois on our way south, two in Nashville, and another in Tina's hometown of Brentwood, Tennessee.

In Knoxville, we were all hosted in style at the home of a friend who invited us, Bill Haslam. Bill's such a basball nut that he actually has a batting cage in his back yard—a man after my own heart. But what the kids made the most of was his big back-yard swimming pool, complete with diving board and jacuzzi.

Knoxville had a brand-new youth baseball complex as nice as the one in Williamsport, Pennsylvania, where they play the Little League World Series each year. And the place was packed that weekend with fans who'd come with their teams from all over the Southeast.

We'd come farther than any other team in the tournament and were the only minority team playing. We looked like real underdogs when we showed up for our first game against some select traveling team decked out in blue uniforms and matching blue baseball gloves. And we'd even forgotten to pack our purple uniform socks.

Our opponents had arrived in a caravan of motor homes full of supporters. The only fans we brought to cheer for us were the coaches—and one uncle who made the trip.

But we weren't without friends. Just before our game, a man walked up and handed a bag of purple baseball socks he'd rushed off and bought when he saw us warming up without any. We were still warming up when another coach walked up with another bag of socks and laughingly asked, "Who beat me to it?"

The folks in Knoxville showed us southern hospitality at its best. They were buying our kids meals and giving them baseball gloves and bats. But I think we showed them something as well.

Our underdogs won one game and lost another on Saturday. And we were scheduled the next day to play the first Sunday game a Near West Little League team had ever played. When we arrived at the park at eight that morning, it was obvious no one had pro-vided for any kind of Sunday morning worship. So before we warmed up, we took our team into the outfield and had our own service.

We sang a few songs together. Then, given the baseball juggernauts we were up against that day, I asked a couple of the boys to read the Bible's account of the story of David and Goliath. I led in prayer. And we closed with the boys belting out a rousing rendition of "Our God Is an Awesome God." When we finished, I looked around and noticed for the first time how many people had seen what we were doing and had gathered around to share in our service. Some of them were crying.

But the most moving experience of that trip for me came on the way home when we pulled off the interstate to eat at a Cracker Barrel restaurant. While we waited for our table, our players naturally wandered around the store.

Suddenly Jason, our catcher and our team's MVP of the tournament, was tugging at my arm. "Coach Bob, Coach Bob. Can I borrow seventy-nine cents?"

I wasn't surprised Jason was out of money. He had as tough a life as any kid on the team. While we'd been in Knoxville, Chrissy Haslam, our host's wife, provided paper and envelopes for all the boys. We instructed them to write a letter home to their moms or grandmothers. Jason didn't have any family member to write to. His mom was in prison. He was living with a teacher from the parochial school he attended—St. Gregory's. So he had written a letter to Tina, telling her what all we'd done since we'd left Chicago and thanking her for lending me and our batboy sons to the team for a whole week.

"What do you need seventy-nine cents for?" I asked him.

"You'll see," he grinned as he took the money.

He was back a couple of minutes later and handed me a bag. "For you to give Tina when you get home."

I pulled out a little hand-carved wooden plaque that said, "You're not just my wife, you're my best friend." I turned the plaque over and saw the price tag: $5.49. With tax it would have been $5.79. He'd asked me for only seventy-nine cents. Which meant Jason had spent the last five dollars of his own money on a gift for me to give to my wife to thank her for letting me share that week's experience with him. *What could I say?!*

Tina and I still have that plaque sitting on her desk at home.

HOLLYWOOD
HARDBALL

If you bear to hear the truth you've spoken,
Twisted by knaves to make a trap for fools.
Or watch the things you gave your life to broken
And stoop to build them up with worn out tools.

Rudyard Kipling, "If"

One day in the spring of 2000, I got a phone call at my office from a friend in New York. "Hey, Bob! I read in the paper that they're making your movie."

"What movie?" I asked, waiting for the punch line.

"About your Little League. I guess Keanu Reeves is going to play you."

Yeah, right! A Hollywood pretty boy playing me. This had to be some sort of joke. So I played along. "I only wish they could have found a more handsome guy; you know, to make the movie more realistic."

It turned out my friend wasn't kidding. "I'll fax you a copy of the article," he promised.

Before he could, my phone rang again. "Hi, Bob, just heard about the movie." And then again, "Congratulations on the movie, man!"

I got maybe a dozen phone calls from friends anxious to tell me what they'd just learned. Every one of them was excited about "your movie." And everyone pretty much reacted the same way as we talked: bewildered that I'd known nothing about it; surprised when I said I'd had nothing to do with it; and absolutely flabbergasted that neither I nor the league had ever signed a release, given our permission for the story to be told, or received a cent from any movie deal or from the book the movie was supposedly going to be based on.

I wasn't too concerned at first. My attitude was more like, "I don't have time to deal with this. Baseball season's here and my plate's kinda full right now."

But then I saw the various clippings friends started sending me. They came from an assortment of print and internet sources, but they all seemed to have been based on the same source in *Variety*. Because they all said pretty much the same thing as this excerpt from www.movie-page.com/news/00/april3-9, htm:

> Keanu Reeves has committed to star for Paramount Pictures in "Hardball," a drama about an inner-city Little League baseball team to be directed by Brian Robbins ("Ready to Rumble"). According to Variety, Reeves will play a baseball coach in the film.... The story is being adapted by screenwriter John Gatins, who co-wrote the Robbins-directed "Varsity Blues."

(In *Varsity Blues,* high school football players, coaches, girls, parents, a rabbi, Mohammed, and Jesus are all mocked, although it has nothing whatsoever to do with the plot. The only African-American character to speak in the movie spews profanity in the few lines he has.)

A number of the articles said the movie *Hardball* was "based on a true story" in Chicago. Some went on to describe the plot. Again from www.movie-page.com:

> In the film, Reeves will play an aimless young man who is scalping tickets, gambling and drinking while his friends are settling down and making money at good jobs. When he tries for the umpteenth time to borrow money from a friend, the pal makes the loan conditional on the guy coaching a Little League team from the Cabrini-Green housing projects in Chicago, a

squad that his brokerage house is sponsoring. The man is transformed by mentoring the kids and finds salvation through the experience.

Aha! The creative genius of Hollywood at work again.

Then someone sent me a copy of a *New York Post* article in which Keanu Reeves talked about his upcoming movie, *Hardball*. About the young black children being portrayed in the movie, Reeves said, "I hope they let them talk the way they really talk. Let them swear. It will be an R-rated picture.... It's a film about both the kids and [Reeves' character] saving each other."

Uh-oh. An actor who lives in luxury hotels is about to tell the world how "they" (nine- to twelve-year-old Chicago Little Leaguers) "really talk."

Somebody sent us a copy of the script. I don't flinch too easily, but a quick review of the screenplay confirmed the worst. The dialog I saw was definitely R-rated. And the worst of it came from the mouths of the young players. In the ten years I'd laughed and cried, lived and died with Chicago Little Leaguers, I'd never been addressed or heard any other coach addressed with such profanity from any African-American Chicago Little Leaguer, let alone a little nine-year-old like one of the recurring characters in the script.

Of course I've heard kids use bad language when they got angry. But never directed at an adult. And never in addressing me or any of our other coaches. I told Tina, "There is no way they would even think of putting that dialog in the mouths of white children in a Little League movie!"

Now that I'd seen the script, Reeves' quote was certainly telling: "Let them talk the way they really talk. Let them swear." The fact that he—and no doubt the writers, the director, and the producers—seemed to believe their script represented cutting-edge realism evidenced not just glaring ignorance but what struck me as an unconscionable prejudice.

When we voiced our concerns about the movie, Paramount dismissed them and insisted, "While inspired by a true story, it's purely a work of fiction." And yet, if Reeves was starring in the picture, presumably the movie would center around his character.

One quick flip through the screenplay left no doubt: Keanu Reeves' character was the movie's prime focus. Reeves plays Conor O'Neil, an Irish drunk who coaches an all-black Little League team sponsored by a securities firm. The field where they play is on Chicago's Near West Side. A closer read showed him as a coach with a continuing drinking problem, a dishonest, self-centered, wild-living rogue who gets in a drunken bar fight and cuts his hand, talks to a priest, takes his team to a White Sox game, drives a station wagon, discusses his deceased father, speaks at one of his player's funerals, then has a catharsis in the film's last moments.

Man, that sounds familiar.

The Catholic school that some of Keanu's players attend, St. Malachy's, is on Oakley Boulevard. *Wow! I live on Oakley.* Our Little League vice-president, Andre, taught there. His father still works there. And some of our NWLL players actually attend there.

In the screenplay, the players refer to a female teacher at St. Malachy's in extremely foul language. When the school's administration expressed concern about this, the production firm told them the film would be shot with and without offensive language. *Great!*

Al Carter called me when he heard about the movie. "That cat's you, man. The movie's about you!" he laughed. But I showed him where it was about him too. Director Brian Robbins' own website stated, "His next project will be *Hardball,* which tells the story of strained relations between two men who create a little league." I showed Al my copy of the script, which actually included a scene in which his real name was used to refer to a league official. Evidently an earlier version of the screenplay used our names, and when they changed it, the writers missed one of the references to "Al." He just shook his head in disgust and said no one connected with the movie had contacted him either.

A firestorm of protest and publicity erupted as the movie production team began shooting on location in Chicago. An August 31 *Chicago Sun-Times* article headlined "Hey Keanu, Clean Up Your Movie!" began:

> A movie about North Side Little Leaguers starring Keanu Reeves is under fire from Mayor Daley and Public Schools CEO Paul Vallas, who say Hollywood has turned a good story about Chicago into a foul-mouthed tale.
>
> Daley wants references to Chicago removed because he says the movie wrongly shows kids shouting four-letter words at volunteer coaches who have been forced by their companies to help out.
>
> Vallas is upset that children are being taken out of school to appear in the film and recite lines often laced with rough language. "It's the 'Clockwork Orange' version of 'The Bad News Bears,'" Vallas said....
>
> Vallas and others who said they have obtained portions of the script said the language used by the children is offensive and graphic, and the movie reinforces negative stereotypes.... Vallas said ... "The movie industry needs to be a little more responsible."
>
> Paramount Pictures, which is making the film, released a statement saying the movie "is a dramatic work of fiction. While it is inspired by real events, all of the characters ... are fictional."

The same day, the *Chicago Tribune* carried an article headlined "Language in 'Hardball' Script Strikes Out with the Real League." That article took a little different slant by beginning:

> In Bob Muzikowski's Loop office, Little League team photos cover almost every surface. The 40-plus Little League teams that Muzikowski has helped establish around Chicago are

fielded with poor kids from Chicago's public housing develop-
ments, including Rockwell Gardens, Henry Horner, and
Cabrini-Green.

Now Muzikowski fears the reputation of one of the
nation's largest urban Little Leagues—not to mention the thousands of dollars corporate sponsors donate each year—is
threatened by the upcoming Paramount movie "Hardball,"
starring Keanu Reeves. The production, now being filmed just
east of 14th Street and Ashland Avenue, is being billed by
company executives as a dramatic work of fiction, inspired by
[a] ... non-fiction book about the program....

But Paramount's fiction-reality split is too narrow for
Muzikowski, who says he obtained a script. He and other
league coaches, including program co-founder Al Carter, con-
tend the script's story line is too close to the real thing, yet filled
with offensive stereotypes about profanity-spouting players.

Despite all of our concerns and the ongoing protests, and even
despite the concerns others expressed on our behalf, no one from
Paramount and no officials from the set listened to our complaints
or even agreed to talk with us before they finally packed up and
left town. But the production wasn't finished. Since the White Sox
had declined Paramount's request to shoot a scene in Comiskey
Park, the crew went on to Detroit to capture a major league ballpark setting in old Tiger Stadium. While they were there, I got a
phone call from a friend saying he'd read all about me that day in
a Detroit paper. The October 26 Associated Press wire story distributed around the country said, "Actor Keanu Reeves was in
town to film scenes for a movie called 'Hardball' on Thursday
night and Friday at the Detroit Tigers' old home.... The story
is ... about playing and coaching Little League baseball amid the
violence of Chicago's Cabrini-Green housing project. Reeves plays
Bob Muzikowski, a former addict turned devout Christian, who
coaches a Little League baseball team."

In the aftermath of all the newspaper publicity, the former assistant Little League coach who wrote the book flew all the way in from his home in Alaska. In the *Chicago Tribune,* he stated he was "comfortable with any screenwriting liberties and that political confrontation would not serve the children."

Easy to say when you reside closer to the Arctic Circle than to any Chicago housing project.

A little later, during an interview aired on Chicago's National Public Radio station WBEZ, he stated, "My book focused on the kids. The movie is focused on a coach, and one particular coach, and the coach's story."

Hmm. If the film is "based on a true story," I wonder which coach?

My concern isn't just how I'm portrayed but that any movie based on the screenplay we read could be very dangerous to all of us who coach in the leagues. You see, we have over six hundred kids in our Little League, and almost every night, our coaches drop their players off in some pretty rough locations. Unlike Keanu and some of the other movie people, we don't have bodyguards or armed security.

So far we haven't needed it. Right now, all the guys working the doors of these buildings, the guys wearing the same color clothes and hats, they kinda like us. Most of the local gang members think it's great that we're out playing ball with their little brothers, nephews, and cousins. But how are they going to feel about us if they see a movie, "based on a true story," about a baseball league in Chicago, exactly like ours, but where selfish white coaches get paid to be bad examples and where a hungover white coach curses and shoves a black Little Leaguer?

Thinking about that makes me want to write Keanu Reeves a letter saying, "Hey buddy! Could you do us a favor? When your movie comes out, would you come back here and drive our Little

League van to drop kids off in the projects after the night games? And while you're doin' that, could our coaches come and hide under your bed in the Four Seasons?"

Perhaps the saddest commentary on this whole sorry movie business is what I saw this spring when I went back to the site where all the game scenes for *Hardball* had been filmed. I drove right past the address where, just after the movie crew pulled out of town, some maniacs in ski masks walked in on a Saturday afternoon, doused the counter with gasoline, and torched the place, leaving the store's two women employees to burn to death. I turned into an alley that wound between buildings, dodging loose bricks and potholes, until I reached the location which had been crowded with high-tech production equipment and swarming with actors, extras, and film-crew workers when we'd been there demonstrating just a few months before.

No trace of that Hollywood limelight remained in that once-again-empty space in the middle of the projects. The bleachers, the fence, and the scoreboard were gone. The base paths had almost filled in with weeds. Even the backstop had been dismantled and hauled off. The moviemakers had come and gone, leaving nothing behind, not even a makeshift ball diamond.

So a few of us went back again with a bag of baseball equipment and started playing catch . . .

GET IN THE GAME

The prosperity of the 1990s not only altered the landscape of inner-city Chicago; it even trickled down and affected the Little League. While our Near West Little League neighborhood has seen significant change, the original Near North Little League location in Cabrini-Green is almost unrecognizable.

The Oscar Mayer factory behind home plate is gone—replaced by half-million-dollar townhouses. Where the fried chicken restaurant stood on Orleans is now an impressive fountain on a lush green lawn encircled by wrought iron fencing. The old brick church has been replaced by a magnificent thirty-foot clock. The basketball courts across the street at Sedgwick and Division have become a parking lot for an upscale shopping center complete with a Blockbuster and Starbucks. "Snipe Tower," the highrise perch from which shooters sometimes used our outfield for evening target practice, has just been demolished.

As for Carson Field itself, real estate developers have turned it back into a wasted, weed-strewn city block. In '98, they had construction crews close off the ballfields, citing plans for more expensive new condos. But it's been three years, three baseball seasons, and up till now, all they've done on the sealed-off baseball diamonds has been to move a little dirt around with bulldozers. The backstops and faded empty infields are still there. The NNLL has eight remaining Little League boys teams and four Little League girls softball teams. They now play on one small field in Old Town.

The only good news is that the condemnation of Carson Field has forced all the remaining age-thirteen-and-over teams in the Near North Little League to commute south and west to play in the NWLL since '98. Which means I get to see lots of familiar faces at Altgeld Park and watch Paul O'Connor and the Zulus finish as runner-up every year. Paul and Holly have coached ten years now and never won a title. Maybe it's the Columbia University sports legacy.

On the West Side, we've also witnessed an influx of new neighbors. Some have moved over from Cabrini—when buildings get demolished, people have to go somewhere. But we have a growing number of yuppies moving into our neighborhood as well. Some of them are wonderful, but most are what I call "non-neighbors." When you meet them on the sidewalk, they are usually wearing a Walkman and have an inside-out sandwich bag on their hand. This bag is used as a pooper-scooper for their guard dog—*if* anybody is looking when Fido relieves himself on the Little League infield. If nobody is looking, the baggie goes unused and we have to clean up after their dog. So while there may be fewer used condoms, needles, and crack vials, now there's Fido too.

I read an article not long ago in *Philanthropy Today* about a team of sociologists at one of our nation's leading universities who had just completed a major two-year, $500,000 research study on urban issues and problems. Their conclusion? Good neighbors make good neighborhoods.

I couldn't help but laugh. *It took two years and a half-a-million-dollar research project to figure that out? Come on.* I could have told them that for a cup of coffee at the nearest Starbucks. But I also could have told them that making a neighborhood "good" doesn't just mean more people and more money moving in. You can end up with a homogeneous group of people who will certainly know what time it is when they buy their grande latte to go home and watch Blockbuster DVDs across the street from an abandoned Little League field.

Once again baseball is the only game in town come springtime in Chicago—ever since Michael Jordan retired. We live just eight blocks from the United Center, and we still play a lot of our Little League games on a field at the western edge of the United Center parking lot.

During the Jordan era, I couldn't get near a Bulls ticket for kids who live around the United Center and play in our league. Frankly, New York immigrants like me kinda got "Bulled out" during the '90s. But lately I've been receiving calls like this: "Hey, Bob. You still work with those inner-city kids? How about bringing a group to the skybox for the Bulls versus the Vancouver Grizzlies next week?" Of course we go even though the Bulls are a lot closer to 12-70 than the 70-12 record posted during the Jordan era.

Despite the decline of Da Bulls, at least two hundred nights every year, twenty thousand visitors (mostly white suburbanites) drive in and out of our neighborhood to the United Center for basketball, hockey, and big-name concerts. When I'm invited to some company or client function in one of the arena's luxury boxes, I'm probably the only person in the place who walks east to get there.

The year before one of these United Center get-togethers, a business colleague tragically killed a girl in a drunk driving accident. (More than sixteen thousand Americans die violently this way every year.) But what strikes me as ironic is that people in that skybox were sadly shaking their heads and solemnly discussing the tragedy . . . while having "one (or several more) for the road." I was the only one *walking* home and one of the only ones not drinking.

Meanwhile, other luxury box guests who learn I live nearby ask me questions such as, "Aren't you worried about crime in the city?" "Why do so many inner-city people continue to break the law?" Then these questioners, with blood-alcohol levels far above the legal limit, proceed to exit the parking lot and speed through the neighborhood for several blocks before they manage to find an expressway entrance-ramp to head for home.

Some fans used to visit the hookers who set up camp on corners outside the arena. But since the city vice squads made a concerted effort to clean up the area for the 1996 Democratic National Convention, low-priced prostitutes don't work on Madison Street as much. They've been replaced today by twenty-nine pages (count 'em) of escort services advertising in the 2001 Chicago Yellow Pages. So while drunk driving and dial-up prostitution services are ignored, the neighborhood guy selling a gram of coke is rousted and handcuffed to the fence.

Think about it. White people break the law in Chicago every day, and we ignore it. Black people break the law, and the prisons overflow.

Can you imagine the reaction if twenty thousand city people went "partying" in the same suburban Barrington neighborhood two hundred nights a year? And if we urinated in their driveways and honked our horns driving down their street at midnight after a long night of drinking? The National Guard would be called out.

Many times I've seen the not-so-subtle face of racism in my neighborhood. Never looking out from under a KKK hood, but often looking out *over* the hood of some late-model luxury car.

I think again of our NWLL field at Touhy Herbert Park next to the United Center parking lot. Despite, or maybe because of, all the neighborhood kids often milling around the park, Bulls and Blackhawks fans or concertgoers seldom even slow down for the stop sign at that corner. I can't count the number of times I've stood at the crosswalk, equipment bag over my shoulder, uniformed team members lined up behind me, waiting for one car to stop and let us get to the other side. Whenever a car does stop, or if we finally catch an opening and a line of cars has to wait for us to file across the street, you can actually hear the sound of electric door locks being activated, *click . . . click . . . click . . .* Granted, we're usually carrying baseball bats on the way to our Little League field, but what do the door locks say to you if you're a ten-year-old black kid?

For those *en route* to the courtside seats, their BMWs and Mercedes are like mobile gated communities. "I've got it. You don't. Stay out."

They say where you stand depends on where you sit. From where I'm sitting, racism is alive and well.

Here's a classic. During football season a year ago, I got to the office early one Monday to find Darron Kirkman's sister Joanne, who works for me as a secretary, waiting for me. She'd obviously been crying.

"What's wrong?"

"It's Jeff!" Jeff Clay is Joanne and Darron's younger step-brother. "He got arrested Saturday night out in River Forest."

"Jeff?" He'd played Little League for me and was in a high school now. A big, sweet, fun-loving teddy bear of a kid who didn't even drink. He'd never been in trouble before. "What happened?"

"They say he robbed somebody."

"Where is he now?"

"Cook County Jail." That wasn't good. Joanne told me what she knew. Sounded like a crazy, mixed-up story to me. But I placed some phone calls to see what I could do. Then Jeff called collect from jail. I had him tell me what happened.

Jeff's football team had played out in the near western suburbs Friday night, and four of the guys got invited to a party following the game. Afterward, since none of them knew their way around River Forest, they got a little turned around and became lost. They were maybe twenty blocks off the Eisenhower when they finally spotted a convenience store where they could get directions back to the interstate.

They were typical teenage boys (not to mention linemen) who hadn't had anything to eat for at least twenty minutes. The whole crew decided to seize the opportunity to purchase additional nourishment. The boys piled out of the car and headed *en masse* toward the door of the store just as a frail, elderly white gentleman shuffled out. Startled to see four hulking black teenagers coming toward him in the dark, the man got so flustered and frightened he suddenly thrust out his hand and said, "Here! Take it. This is all I have."

One of the boys instinctively took what the man handed him—a dollar and a small cigarette lighter. The old guy then went rushing off around the side of the store. The boys, shaking their heads and laughing about the strange exchange, went on inside.

They each ordered a slurpee and a couple of hot dogs, which they heated up in the store's microwave. They took a few more minutes to put ketchup and mustard on the dogs, pay the tab, and ask directions. Then just as they sauntered out of the store, three police cars wheeled into the parking lot with their lights flashing. "Hands up! Get against the car!" They were handcuffed, hauled off to jail, and charged with the aggravated robbery of the old man, who'd rushed home and called the cops about the black gang who'd mugged him.

"But we never robbed him, Bob. We never touched him. That crazy old man just handed us the money!"

I called a lawyer, told him the story, wrote a check for his initial fee, and had Joanne deliver it. Bond was set at ten grand. So I had to put up a thousand (Jeff's family didn't have that kind of money) and we had him out before the day was over. He came straight to my office, still shaken and scared. The lawyer talked to the police, and somebody talked to the old man, who eventually admitted the boys' story made sense and maybe it had been a big misunderstanding. Within ten days or so, all charges were dropped.

Naturally, the bondsman kept 10 percent of my thousand. Plus I was out the lawyer's fee. But that seemed a small price to pay for keeping an innocent kid out of jail.

In my neighborhood, stories such as Jeff's are not uncommon. And unless a kid like Jeff has a neighbor or knows somebody who has a few resources and can make the right connections, he might end up in prison for a long time.

It's 10:30 at night when the doorbell rings. Two boys are standing on my front steps. One is nine; the other ten. "Coach Bob, we locked out."

They aren't on my team. I don't even know them by name. But they have Little League uniforms on. And I've got a Bible on my desk. What do I say? Go away? Stay somewhere else tonight? Show me that Bible verse.

Guess what? The next morning, the boys haven't disappeared. They are still there. And they're real hungry. So I stay and help Tina get everybody together for breakfast. I'm happy to do it, but shoot, it means I'll be late for my first appointment.

End result, a client may judge me "overcommitted" or even "unreliable." Ouch. Thank God my father left me this quote from "the King": "The ultimate measure of a person is not where they stand in moments of comfort and convenience but where they stand at times of challenge and controversy."

You never know when those inconvenient challenges are going to crop up. Last summer, my shortstop's mother dropped him off for practice one afternoon and never came back to pick him up. He lived with us and his aunt for the rest of the summer before we were finally able to locate some relatives who could take him.

Lots of people today bemoan the breakdown of the family. Where does the next generation learn about marriage and family values? From their families. And if they have only a very dysfunctional one, a neighbor's family might be the example they need.

I know there is no one big magic solution to the complex issues facing urban communities today. But there are five hundred or five thousand little solutions that can add up.

But you gotta be there. You can't tell people what they should do when you are "geographically unavailable" to help.

I think we all might need to do a little soul-searching. I mean, if we're going to church and singing that "I Surrender All" hymn, something's got to give.

We've supposedly heard what the Bible says. We've read Jesus' teaching about loving our neighbors. And in America's churches, we have more resources than any nation in history.

So why aren't we doing more in our cities? How come all Christians making x-amount of dollars live clustered together with other Christians who also make x-amount of dollars? They weren't planted there.

Christians buy their children WWJD (What Would Jesus Do?) bracelets. Yet they choose to live where it's safest and best for themselves. Proximity to any kind of need is viewed as a negative.

The words "Do not fear" are found 366 times in the Bible. "Fear not." The bad guys will always get tired before the good guys.

We saw this when we moved into our West Side neighborhood. We planted flowers; they ripped them up. We planted again and they ripped them up. About the third time, somebody else on the block planted flowers, and finally we've ended up with a tree-lined street.

What we need on the West Side of Chicago, what we need more of in every urban neighborhood in America, are people willing to get in the game. To get involved.

Jesus didn't say, "When you've paid someone to do it unto the least of these . . ." And he didn't even say, "When you've prayed for someone doing it unto the least of these . . ." What he said was, "When *you* have done it unto the least of these, *you* have done it unto me."

Professing Christians could be the most powerful, best-connected "gang" in America today, capable of providing those resources and being the connection to other resources that millions of disenfranchised people need. If we really want to change our cities, what we need most are more talented, bright, confident people with resources to move in, dig in, and get seriously, personally invested in our city neighborhoods.

Is it inconvenient? Are you late to work sometimes? Sure. But look, when the Good Samaritan picked the man up, put him on his donkey, took him to the nearest hotel, asked the manager to clean him up and care for his needs, it cost him more than the money. He was probably late to his next appointment, and he may have even lost the business. That's what it's really all about, isn't it? He might have lost the business.

He could have avoided all that by simply saying, "I'm not called to help the guy beat up on the side of the road. I'm called to be a Christian businessman."

But he didn't. He stopped. He got involved. And by doing so, he became the most famous example of "the good neighbor" in the best-selling book of all time.

LAST LICKS

Spring is in the air. At least for some of us.

Here in Orlando, we just read that the Chicago Cubs game was postponed because of snow yesterday.

For thirty former Near West Little Leaguers, however, the forecast is sunny, high in the low eighties. We're in Florida attending the Doyle Baseball School inside the spring training home of the Atlanta Braves—Disney's Wide World of Sports. Yeah, I can't quite believe we're here either.

The thirty players represent our two West Side neighborhood high schools—the Manley Wildcats and the Crane Cougars. I coached some of these young men when they were eleven and twelve. So I'm relishing the growth and progress I see.

Both Manley and Crane had quit fielding baseball teams prior to the inception of the Near West Little League. But their programs have been revived by our former players and four dedicated Little League coaches who teach at those schools—Rory Clay, John Deligiannis, Joe McDermott, and David Penn. This spring-break trip is sponsored by six business guys—four of my Christian

255

friends, me, and perhaps the NWLL's biggest fan, Ken Alpart. Ken is not only one of my best friends; he's my marathon running partner. We have committed to discuss both politics and religion (his Judaism and my faith in the North African Jew, Jesus Christ), just to make sure we are really friends.

The Doyle Baseball School is not a camp. As former New York Yankee World Series hero Brian Doyle would say, "Camp is for roasting marshmallows." This is 6:00 A.M. wake-up, 6:30 A.M. breakfast, 7:15 A.M. bus, 8:00 A.M. chapel, 8:30 A.M. to 3:00 P.M. drill, drill, drill. After that, it's party time at the pool and theme parks.

This evening, I am sitting on the balcony of the hotel with a great view of the parking lot. Beneath us, some of the players are doing drills on their own. That's a good sign. I'm discussing the day with my eight- and nine-year-old sons, who made the trip with me, when Jonathan Hayes approaches us.

Jonathan plays first base for Manley and was the starting center and noseguard on their football team. He's a big burly guy. We ate breakfast together our first day in Florida. When I asked him about his large biceps tattoo, he said, "That's my cousin Sherman Scott. He just turned his life around last year but was shot twice in the back of the head." Before we finished breakfast, I got to see three other players' "tombstone tattoos" in memory of loved ones murdered.

Anyway, Jonathan approaches me up on the balcony.

"Coach Bob. It's great to see you talking with your sons. I never had that. I mean I wished I woulda had that."

His words come unsolicited. But I "knew that he knew."

Several of the thirty high school players on the trip are already fathers. None of them live with the mothers of their children.

This oft-discussed fatherhood factor is the number one issue for many city kids. Say what you want, there are just not enough good men available on a daily basis.

This whole trip has been unforgettable, the workouts, the meals, dancing the Jamaican on Main Street of the Magic Kingdom with the team—all of it. I've really gotten to know the players better this week. I like them a lot. So do my sons.

I just don't want to ever have to get one of those tattoos.

I do see glimmers of hope. At the NWLL finals last year, the Little League Pirates' eight-to-ten-year-olds had a dugout full of fathers and grandfathers cheering their team on. My team had been knocked out of the playoffs two days earlier. But as much as I hate to lose, I had a blast sitting in the stands with nothing to do but enjoy watching the game with a number of old friends.

Duane Bell was back in Chicago for a visit. He's now assistant director of the Bowery Transitional Center in New York City. *He* took *me* to dinner last month for his seventh anniversary of being sober. Duane saves lives every day.

Galen C. was there too. He is still earning a regular paycheck and paying his FICA working as a waiter at one of the restaurants at the Mercantile Exchange. He comes by every once in a while. When he asked if I'd heard from Sam Dillon lately, I told him the Sandman had earned a master's degree out in Iowa and is now a college professor of sociology.

Even Darron Kirkman was back in town for a short visit. Once I told him my "fake it till you make it" secret, it didn't take the guy long. After college graduation and a short run with the Oakland Raiders, he got a white collar job working for Coca-Cola in northern California, where he now lives with his wife and two daughters. We talk on the phone every week.

Dionte, my young second baseman whose mom didn't want to let him escape the insanity to play that day I went to get him in Cabrini, is a senior graduating from high school this year. He was there at the finals last summer. His mom married the white guy who was sitting on the couch that morning years ago. They both got sober. Arnie coaches in the league himself now. The whole family attends our church.

Not all of my friends were sitting in the stands with me watching the finals. One of them was out on the field, calling the game—as usual. We recently helped get Miles his first apartment. He works now as an orderly at a nursing home. And of course, he will umpire two games a night, six days a week, all summer long for the NWLL again this season.

Mike Julian, the guy down at the Living Light farm who couldn't believe how hard the Amish men worked, was also out on the field for the final. He'd learned a few things about working hard himself. Five years ago, he was a drug addict. But he graduated from Bob Weeden's discipleship program at the farm and now runs the Prairie Harvest Bread Kitchen out in Oak Park. Last year, I attended his wedding when he married the mother of his ten-year-old son. They recently had their second baby. In the final, he was coaching his son's team in the NWLL championship game. He and his Angels team were the ones who had eliminated my squad from the playoffs. But I showed him; I helped elect him the new vice president of our league.

As encouraging as it was to look around the field and the stands during last year's championships and realize the impact the leagues have had on so many lives, I knew when I got in the game that you can't win 'em all.

Stanley Kirkman, who is Darron, Joanne, and Jeff's older brother, was a sad reminder of that. Stanley had just gotten out of prison a while back when Darron told me his brother really wanted to go straight and asked me if I could help. After I found him a job working for a drywall contractor I knew, Stanley and his girlfriend actually started coming to church with us. Things seemed to be going great. His boss even called me one Friday night to say Stanley was the best worker he'd ever had.

The following Monday morning, I picked up the paper. Stanley had taken a ride with some buddies to collect on a loan one of his friends had made to some guy out in the suburbs. The guy didn't have the money; there was an argument; Stanley's friend decided to steal some of the guy's stuff as "repayment." The local cops caught them after a thirty-mile expressway chase. Because he was with the friends and his car was used in the robbery, Stanley had violated parole and had once again become "a collect call from a correctional institution."

There's no end to the foolish things some people will do. Other people just don't want to change. I've had my car stolen five times and sold for dope by guys I was trying to help. You really can't win 'em all. At least it keeps me from wasting money on expensive cars.

But for every Anthony Garrett who goes off the deep end and shoots an innocent kid, for every innocent kid like Brian Dixon lost in a senseless tragedy, there are hundreds we can get to know and then help.

Many of our original Little Leaguers still stay in touch. Some of them have finished high school now and are working for former coaches down at the Merc or at the Board of Trade. Others have gone on to college and are scattered around the country.

But the kids aren't the only ones who have benefited from our leagues. So have a lot of us who helped.

Paul and Holly O'Connor not only still coach a team; they continue serving as foster parents to boys who have played for them over the years.

Mike and Kristi Edwards, who met coaching on Carson Field the second Little League season, have been married for eight years and are some of our best supporters. They were there at the finals last year.

So was Joe Guinan, my old fraternity brother, who is now president of Fuji Futures. Joe has provided coaches and sponsored teams in the Near North and Near West leagues since their beginnings and still lives just down the block from me. His wife, Allison, runs the neighborhood parks committee.

You might say Joe's a bit overqualified for the role he played at the finals. But he seemed to be having a good time wearing a Dr. Seuss Cat in the Hat hat and flippin' burgers on the grill.

I still keep in touch with a lot of former coaches, like Bill Vranos, who've moved to other parts of the country. And many of those still in town have become my closest friends.

When I shake the hand of a fellow coach from the Near North, Near West, or East Harlem Little Leagues, it's a different handshake from the one you get with the guy you go golfing with. Something good, something deeper is happening there. We communicate and relate on a different level because of the experiences we've shared.

I found the same thing was true between me and my neighbor Dean Grazier after the Tin Man caper in our alley. We grew to have a different kind of neighborly relationship after I helped Dean put the new gutter up on his garage. Always before, we'd exchanged occasional hellos across the alley. But afterward, we'd cook out together in our yard or his. His dog played with my kids while his wife and Scout fed the pigeons in the alley.

Sometimes Dean and I just looked at each other and laughed, remembering that day with the Tin Man. That following spring, Dean, the retired Wrigley Field groundskeeper, taught me how to really build a pitcher's mound on our Little League fields.

The year after that, he died of cancer. One day not long before he passed away, Dean told me, "I'm really glad you caught that guy, Bob."

But we both always knew that really the Tin Man had caught *us*.

We head east. It's dawn. Peaceful except for an ambulance pulling into the Cook County Hospital ER as we pass.

I'm running with twenty-two-year-old Kenji Conley, one of my original Little Leaguers from my first Pygmy team. He has lived around the corner for the last ten years. He's our neighbor. He and his sister were two of the first kids Tina and I helped attend private schools.

He graduated from private high school and attends the University of Memphis. He is equipment manager for the University of Memphis basketball team under former New Jersey Nets coach John Calipari.

Kenji is getting in shape for the basketball season. Under Calipari, even the equipment manager has to be in shape. We both need the miles.

"Oh man, I can't believe you got us up this early, Bob. I mean, the sun's not even up yet."

"Oh, it's there, Kenji. It's always there. We just can't always see it."

"Man, it's early. It feels good though . . . real good."

"Hey, sleep's overrated. Let's pick it up, Kenji. C'mon. We're gonna catch the sunrise over the lake. This is the best part."

CHICAGO HOPE ACADEMY

Bringing hope to Chicago's youth and communities through a quality non-denominational Christian education.

Vivat Veritas
Let Truth Prevail

Chicago Hope Academy will provide the educational resources necessary for young people with varying backgrounds to live extraordinary lives. It is being designed as a co-educational, independent, college and life preparatory school dedicated to nurturing and challenging the whole person—body, mind, and spirit—to the glory of God.

Chicago Hope Academy
601 South LaSalle Street
Second Floor
Chicago, IL 60605

E-mail: info@chicagohopeacademy.com
www.chicagohopeacademy.com

We want to hear from you. Please send your comments about this book to us in care of the address below. Thank you.

GRAND RAPIDS, MICHIGAN 49530

www.zondervan.com